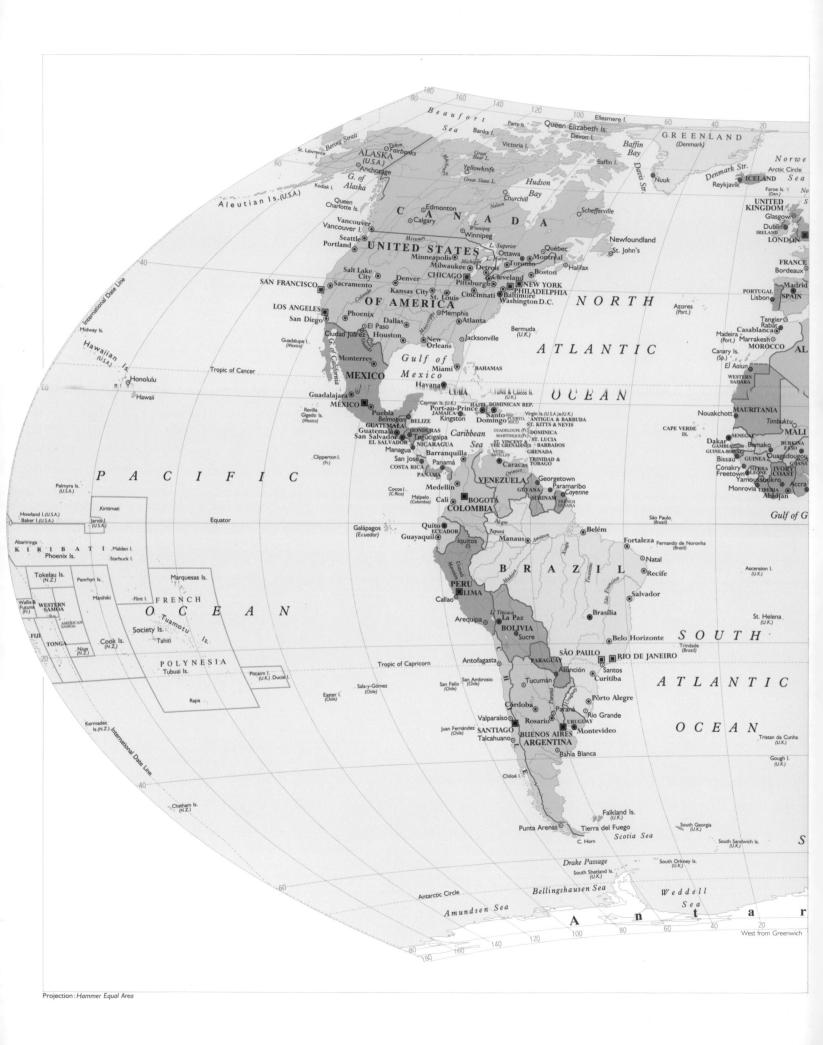

Projection: Hammer Equal Area

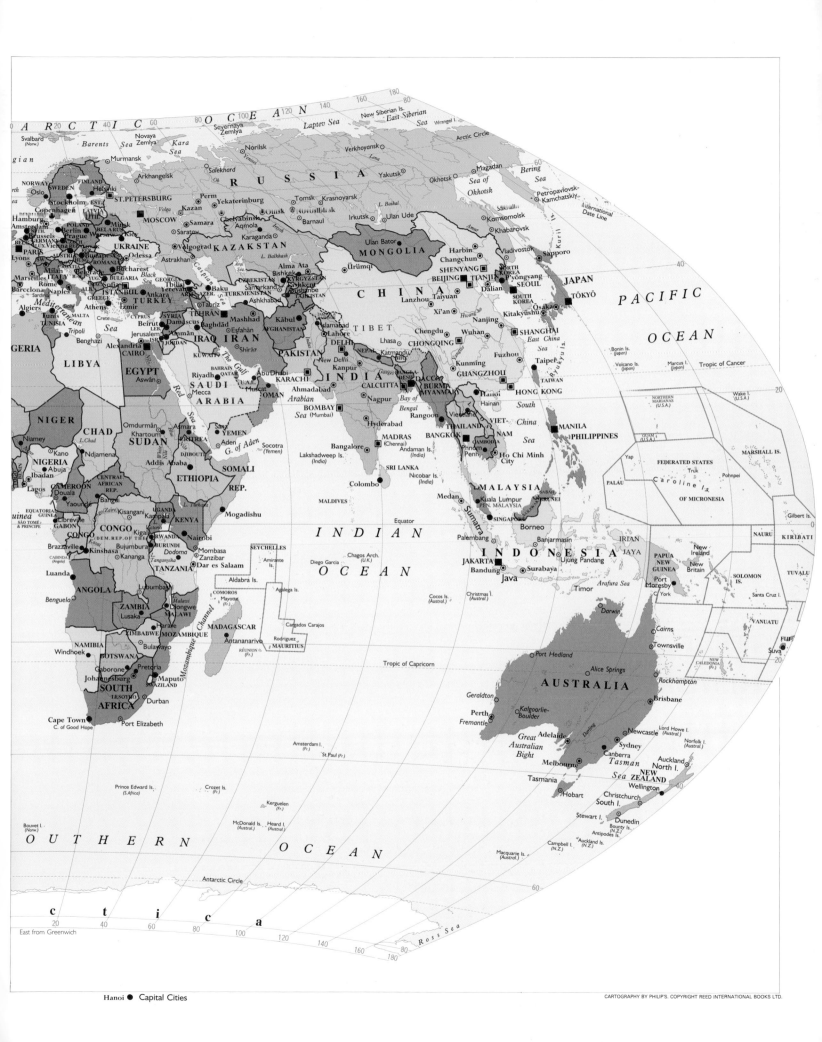

Hanoi ● Capital Cities

PHILIP'S
HISTORY ATLAS

Published in Great Britain by
George Philip Ltd,
an imprint of Reed Consumer Books Ltd,
Michelin House,
81 Fulham Road,
London SW3 6RB
and Aukland and Melbourne

Copyright © 1998 George Philip

ISBN 0-540-07521-3

A CIP catalogue record for this book is available
from the British Library

Printed in China

Editor Jane Edmonds

Assistant editor Jannet King

Cartography by Philip's Map Studio

Additional cartography by Cosmographics, Watford

Cartographic editor Hazell Lintott

Designed by The Design Revolution, Brighton

Picture Credits Front cover
Elizabeth I: Bridgeman Art Library (Philip Mould, Historical Portraits,
London)
Nelson Mandela: Rex Features (Frederick de Klerk)

The map of trench warfare on page 41 is based on a map in
The Atlas of the First World War by Martin Gilbert (1970),
by permission of Routledge

CONTENTS

THE ROMAN EMPIRE

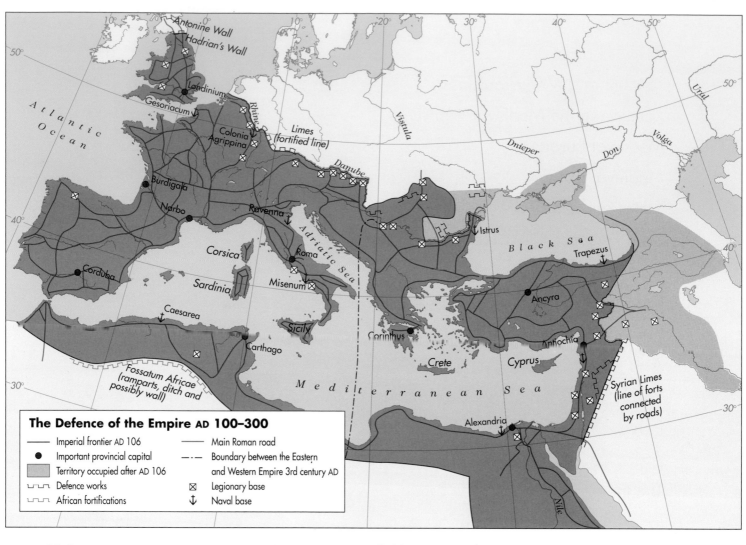

The Defence of the Empire AD 100–300

- —— Imperial frontier AD 106
- ● Important provincial capital
- Territory occupied after AD 106
- ⊔⌐⌐ Defence works
- ⊔⌐⌐ African fortifications
- —— Main Roman road
- ––·–· Boundary between the Eastern and Western Empire 3rd century AD
- ⊠ Legionary base
- ↓ Naval base

In establishing a great empire, which at its peak stretched from Britain in the northwest to Syria in the east, the Romans helped to lay the foundations of European civilisation. Wherever the Roman army established control, science was employed for practical ends, from underfloor heating and watermills, to aqueducts and an impressive road network. The Romans introduced an efficient system of government and a language that was understood everywhere. They also adopted and spread Christianity.

▼ Rome controlled the entire Italian peninsula by 275 BC. It then embarked on a long campaign of conquest, defeating the Carthaginians and Greeks before expanding into northern Europe and Asia.

▲ The Romans defended the frontiers of their empire by building many forts, wooden palisades and walls.

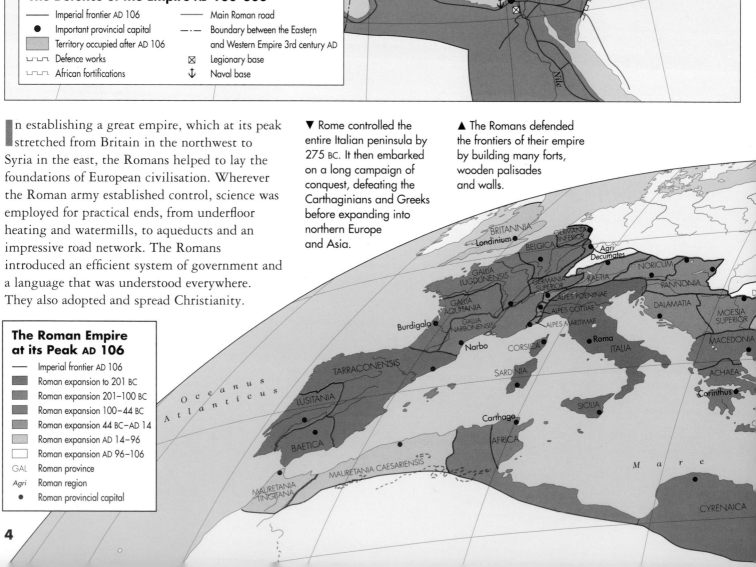

The Roman Empire at its Peak AD 106

- —— Imperial frontier AD 106
- Roman expansion to 201 BC
- Roman expansion 201–100 BC
- Roman expansion 100–44 BC
- Roman expansion 44 BC–AD 14
- Roman expansion AD 14–96
- Roman expansion AD 96–106
- GAL Roman province
- *Agri* Roman region
- ● Roman provincial capital

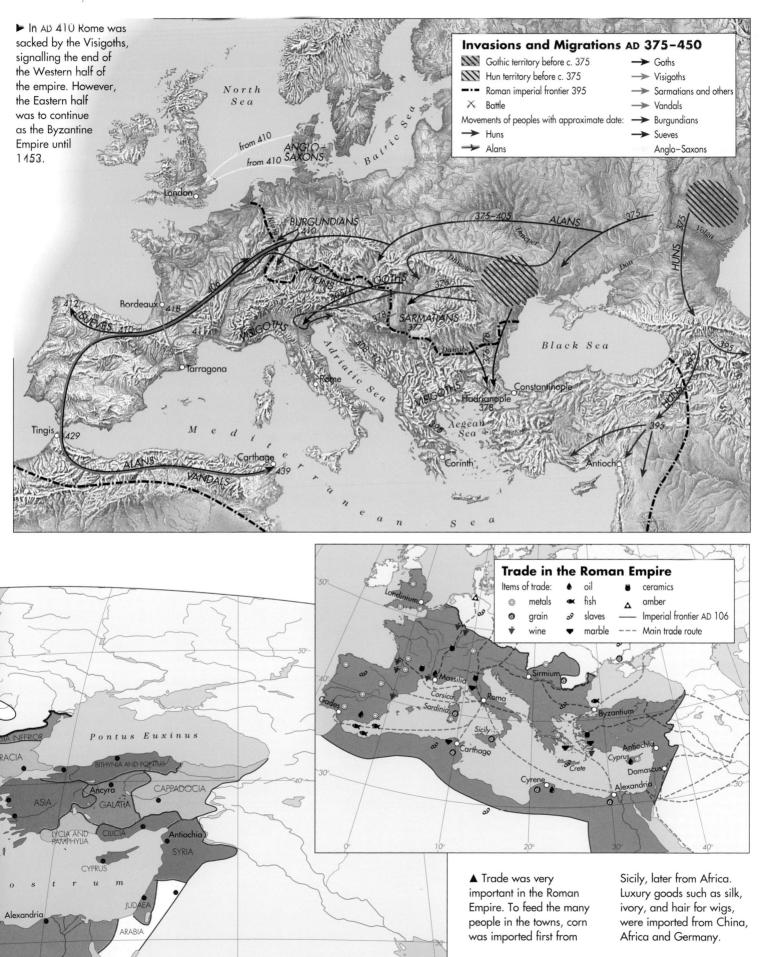

▶ In AD 410 Rome was sacked by the Visigoths, signalling the end of the Western half of the empire. However, the Eastern half was to continue as the Byzantine Empire until 1453.

Invasions and Migrations AD 375–450

- Gothic territory before c. 375
- Hun territory before c. 375
- —·—· Roman imperial frontier 395
- ✕ Battle
- Movements of peoples with approximate date:
- → Huns
- → Alans
- → Goths
- → Visigoths
- → Sarmatians and others
- → Vandals
- → Burgundians
- → Sueves
- → Anglo-Saxons

North Sea

Baltic Sea

from 410 ANGLO-SAXONS
from 410

London

BURGUNDIANS 410

375–405 ALANS 375

Volga

HUNS 375

Dnieper

Dniester

Don

406 HUNS GOTHS 376

Bordeaux 418

412

SUEVES 410 411 VISIGOTHS

SARMATIANS 377

378

Danube

Black Sea

395

Tarragona

408–10

Rome

Adriatic Sea

VISIGOTHS

Hadrianople 378

Constantinople

M e d i t e Tingis 429

Carthage 439

ALANS

VANDALS

Corinth

Aegean Sea

395

Antioch

HUNS

r r a n e a n   S e a

Trade in the Roman Empire

Items of trade:
- ◗ oil
- ❁ metals
- ◆ grain
- ♈ wine
- ▰ ceramics
- ✠ fish
- ∾ slaves
- ▼ marble
- △ amber
- —— Imperial frontier AD 106
- - - - Main trade route

50°

Londinium

50°

Massilia

Corsica

Sirmium

Gades

Sardinia

Roma

Byzantium

40°

Sicily

Antiochia

Carthago

Crete

Cyprus

Damascus

30°

Cyrene

Alexandria

30°

10°   20°   30°   40°

Pontus Euxinus

ASIA INFERIOR

THRACIA

BITHYNIA AND PONTUS

Ancyra

CAPPADOCIA

ASIA

GALATIA

LYCIA AND PAMPHYLIA

CILICIA

Antiochia

CYPRUS

SYRIA

o s t r u m

Alexandria

JUDAEA

ARABIA

AEGYPTUS

▲ Trade was very important in the Roman Empire. To feed the many people in the towns, corn was imported first from Sicily, later from Africa. Luxury goods such as silk, ivory, and hair for wigs, were imported from China, Africa and Germany.

5

ROMAN BRITAIN

A Roman army first invaded Britain in 55 and 54 BC, under the leadership of Julius Caesar. It withdrew after defeating a number of tribes, including the Catuvellauni and Trinovantes, but these tribes continued to pose a threat to the Romans across the English Channel in Gaul. The Romans were also aware that Britain contained many valuable resources, such as tin and iron. Consequently, in AD 43 Emperor Claudius launched a full-scale expedition. The Roman legions experienced only occasional difficulty in dealing with the forces that opposed them, and by AD 60 they controlled England as far north as the River Humber, and by 80 the whole of Wales. The new governor, Agricola, then pushed northwards into Scotland. The Romans found it hard to maintain a presence in Scotland, but they ruled the southern half of Britain for almost 400 years. Much of England became a peaceful province in which many adopted the Roman way of life.

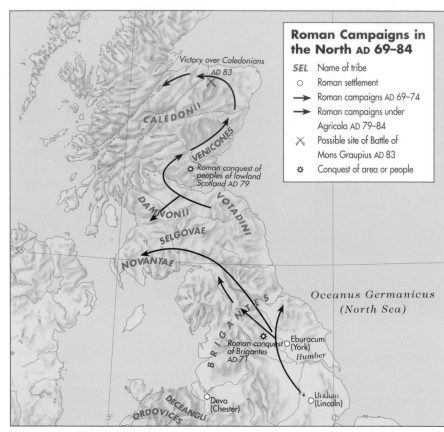

Roman Campaigns in the North AD 69–84

SEL	Name of tribe
○	Roman settlement
→	Roman campaigns AD 69–74
→	Roman campaigns under Agricola AD 79–84
✕	Possible site of Battle of Mons Graupius AD 83
✿	Conquest of area or people

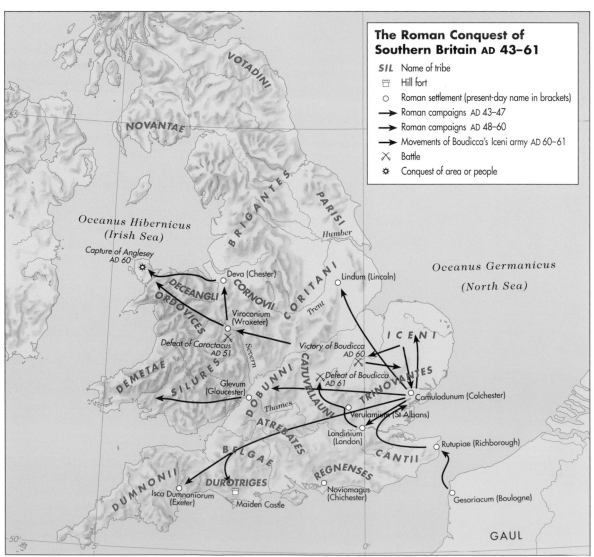

The Roman Conquest of Southern Britain AD 43–61

SIL	Name of tribe
⌂	Hill fort
○	Roman settlement (present-day name in brackets)
→	Roman campaigns AD 43–47
→	Roman campaigns AD 48–60
→	Movements of Boudicca's Iceni army AD 60–61
✕	Battle
✿	Conquest of area or people

▲ Agricola, the Roman governor of Britain between AD 78 and 85, was convinced of the need to conquer Scotland. In 83 he won a great victory over the Caledonians at the Battle of Mons Graupius, thus gaining the whole of lowland Scotland for the empire. The gain, however, was only temporary.

◄ The Roman invasion force in AD 43 consisted of 40,000 men. They marched through southeast England and captured the town of Camulodunum, from where they advanced to the Severn and Trent rivers. They only met with serious resistance when they reached Wales, where Caractacus led the opposing forces until his defeat in 51. By 60 the Romans controlled England as far north as the Humber, but in that year Boudicca, Queen of the Iceni, led a major revolt. The greater armed power of the Romans eventually prevailed, and secured a crushing victory over Boudicca in 61.

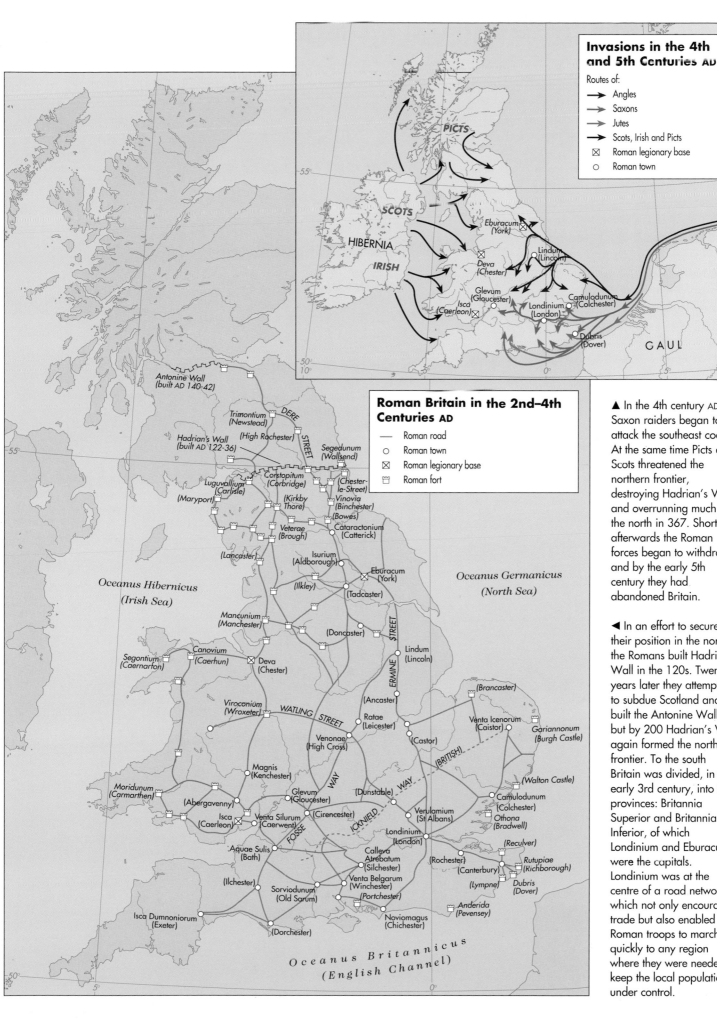

Invasions in the 4th and 5th Centuries AD

Routes of:

→ Angles
→ Saxons
→ Jutes
→ Scots, Irish and Picts
⊠ Roman legionary base
○ Roman town

PICTS

SCOTS

HIBERNIA

IRISH

Eburacum (York)

Lindum (Lincoln)

Deva (Chester)

Glevum (Gloucester)

Camulodunum (Colchester)

Isca (Caerleon)

Londinium (London)

Dubris (Dover)

GAUL

Roman Britain in the 2nd–4th Centuries AD

— Roman road
○ Roman town
⊠ Roman legionary base
⌂ Roman fort

Antonine Wall (built AD 140-42)

Trimontium (Newstead)

DERE STREET

Hadrian's Wall (built AD 122-36)

(High Rochester)

Segedunum (Wallsend)

Luguvallium (Carlisle)

Corstopitum (Corbridge)

(Chester-le-Street)

(Maryport)

(Kirkby Thore)

Vinovia (Binchester)

(Bowes)

Veterae (Brough)

Cataractonium (Catterick)

(Lancaster)

Isurium (Aldborough)

Eburacum (York)

(Ilkley)

(Tadcaster)

Oceanus Hibernicus (Irish Sea)

Mancunium (Manchester)

(Doncaster)

ERMINE STREET

Lindum (Lincoln)

Oceanus Germanicus (North Sea)

Segontium (Caernarfon)

Canovium (Caerhun)

Deva (Chester)

Viroconium (Wroxeter)

WATLING STREET

(Ancaster)

(Brancaster)

Ratae (Leicester)

Venta Icenorum (Caistor)

Gariannonum (Burgh Castle)

Venonae (High Cross)

(Castor)

(BRITISH) WAY

Magnis (Kenchester)

(Walton Castle)

Moridunum (Carmarthen)

(Abergavenny)

Glevum (Gloucester)

(Dunstable)

ICKNIELD WAY

Camulodunum (Colchester)

Isca (Caerleon)

Venta Silurum (Caerwent)

(Cirencester)

Verulamium (St Albans)

Othona (Bradwell)

FOSSE WAY

Aquae Sulis (Bath)

Londinium (London)

(Reculver)

(Ilchester)

Calleva Atrebatum (Silchester)

(Rochester)

(Canterbury)

Rutupiae (Richborough)

Sorviodunum (Old Sarum)

Venta Belgarum (Winchester)

(Portchester)

(Lympne)

Dubris (Dover)

Isca Dumnoniorum (Exeter)

(Dorchester)

Noviomagus (Chichester)

Anderida (Pevensey)

Oceanus Britannicus (English Channel)

▲ In the 4th century AD Saxon raiders began to attack the southeast coast. At the same time Picts and Scots threatened the northern frontier, destroying Hadrian's Wall and overrunning much of the north in 367. Shortly afterwards the Roman forces began to withdraw, and by the early 5th century they had abandoned Britain.

◄ In an effort to secure their position in the north, the Romans built Hadrian's Wall in the 120s. Twenty years later they attempted to subdue Scotland and built the Antonine Wall, but by 200 Hadrian's Wall again formed the northern frontier. To the south Britain was divided, in the early 3rd century, into two provinces: Britannia Superior and Britannia Inferior, of which Londinium and Eburacum were the capitals. Londinium was at the centre of a road network which not only encouraged trade but also enabled Roman troops to march quickly to any region where they were needed to keep the local population under control.

ANCIENT AND MEDIEVAL CHINA

In the 2nd millennium BC large parts of northern China were conquered and ruled by the Shang Dynasty, followed by the Zhou. By the 5th century BC, however, seven major states were competing for control of China. Between 280 and 221 BC the state of Qin eventually achieved supremacy over the others, and King Zheng proclaimed himself 'First Emperor'. His early death provided the Hans with an opportunity to establish a dynasty which was to rule China for over 400 years. During this time China had a population of over 50 million, which was often mobilised for warfare and large public works. Walled cities became the focal points of a trading network that stretched across the empire. A series of peasant revolts hastened the collapse of the Han Empire in AD 220, and it was not until 624 that China was reunited by the Tang Dynasty, ushering in a golden age of expansion and prosperity. The end of the dynasty in 907 heralded another period of disunity until the Song Dynasty was established in 960. The empire over which the Song ruled was constantly under threat from the non-Chinese people to the north, but it survived until 1276 when the whole of China fell to the Mongols.

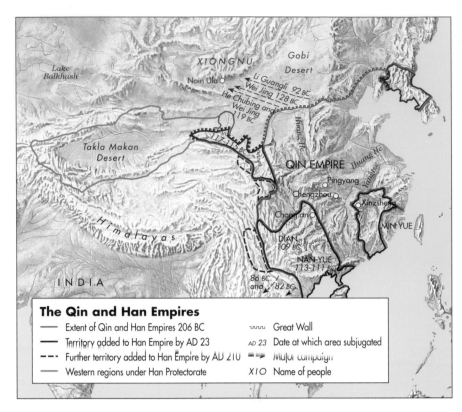

The Qin and Han Empires

—— Extent of Qin and Han Empires 206 BC	⌇⌇⌇ Great Wall
—— Territory added to Han Empire by AD 23	AD 23 Date at which area subjugated
- - - Further territory added to Han Empire by AD 210	➡ Major campaign
—— Western regions under Han Protectorate	XIO Name of people

▲ Both the Qin and Han emperors were determined to expand the frontiers of the lands over which they ruled. They were also determined to keep the nomadic non-Chinese out of the empire, and in the 3rd century BC the Qin emperor joined sections of existing walled defences to create the Great Wall.

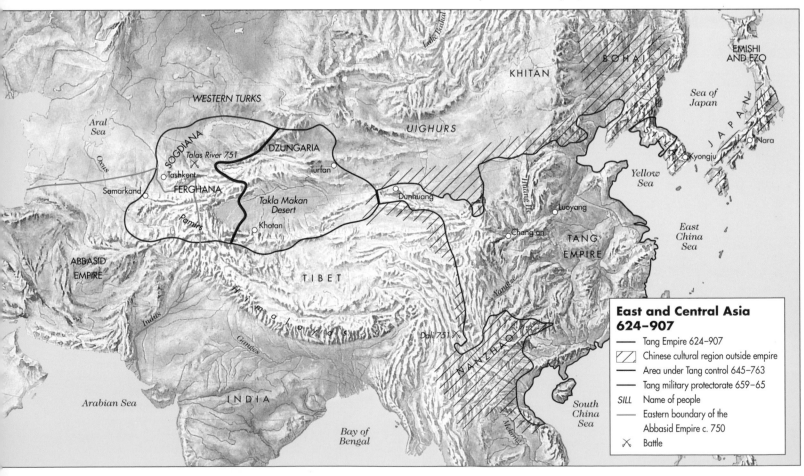

East and Central Asia 624–907

——	Tang Empire 624–907
▨	Chinese cultural region outside empire
——	Area under Tang control 645–763
——	Tang military protectorate 659–65
SILL	Name of people
——	Eastern boundary of the Abbasid Empire c. 750
✕	Battle

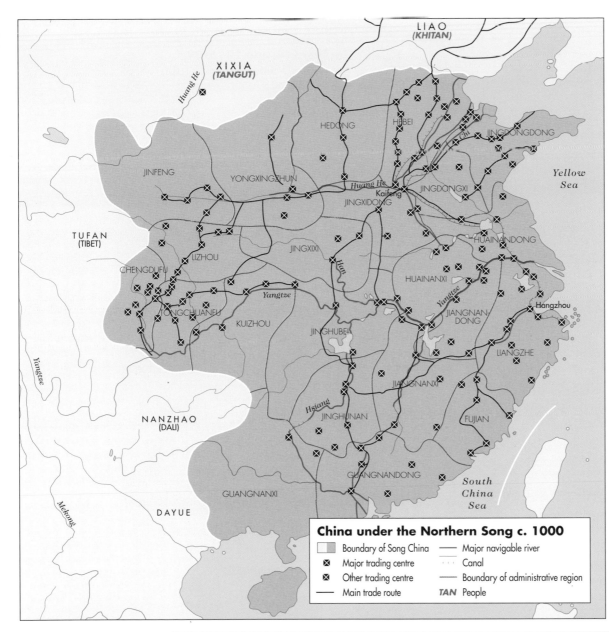

The Chinese Empire over which the Song ruled did not include Central Asia, and on its northern border it faced the hostile states of Liao and Xixia. However, the Song period saw a revival in the native Chinese philosopy of Confucianism. The number of scholar-officials greatly increased, with 400,000 candidates sitting exams each year. Scholarly families fuelled a demand for books, and there were many improvements in printing, including the use of moveable type. New forms of art also flourished with the encouragement of the emperor. Emperor Huizong (r. 1100–26) was blamed for the loss of the north to Jurchen invaders because he allowed his interest in art to distract him from government.

▼ The Song lost the north to a confederation of Jurchen tribes from the mountains of east Siberia in 1127. They then moved their capital from Kaifeng (at the centre of the canal and road network) to Hangzhou. The Jurchen, who established the Jin Dynasty, adopted Kaifeng as their capital in 1161.

China under the Northern Song c. 1000

- Boundary of Song China
- ⊠ Major trading centre
- ⊠ Other trading centre
- — Main trade route
- — Major navigable river
- ⋯ Canal
- — Boundary of administrative region
- **TAN** People

◀ The influence of the Tang Dynasty was felt throughout Asia for almost 300 years. The trade routes of the Silk Road were brought under China's control, and by the mid-7th century the Chinese Empire had reached its greatest extent prior to the conquests of the Manchus 1000 years later. However, in 751 two major defeats were inflicted on the Tang – one by the Arabs at the Battle of Talas River and the other by the Kingdom of Nanzhao at the Battle of Dali. From this point Tang influence began to wane.

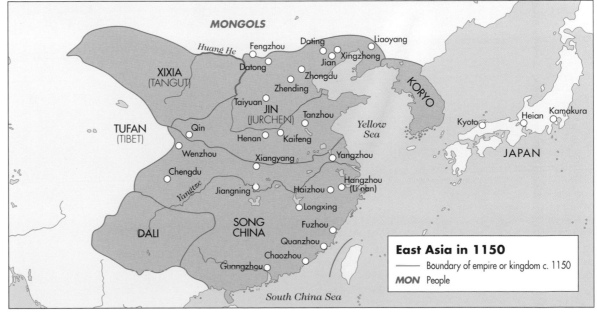

East Asia in 1150

- — Boundary of empire or kingdom c. 1150
- **MON** People

RELIGION IN THE MEDIEVAL WORLD

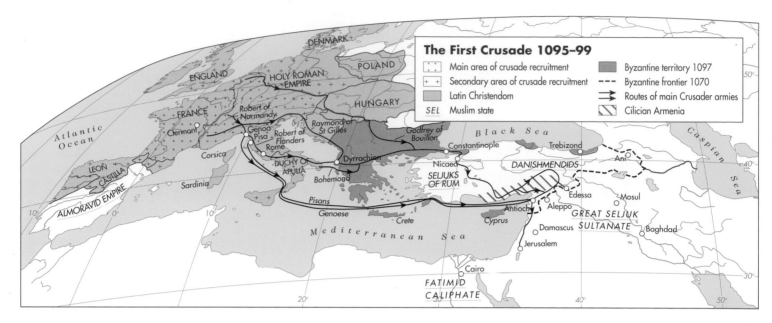

The First Crusade 1095–99

∴	Main area of crusade recruitment
+ +	Secondary area of crusade recruitment
	Latin Christendom
SEL	Muslim state

	Byzantine territory 1097
– – –	Byzantine frontier 1070
→	Routes of main Crusader armies
▨	Cilician Armenia

By the 11th century the Christian world consisted of much of Europe, while the Muslim world stretched from Persia in the east to Spain in the west. It included the Holy Land (Palestine) which, towards the end of the century, the Christians in Western Europe became intent on recapturing. In 1095 Pope Urban II launched the First Crusade and an expedition of perhaps 100,000 people set out for the Holy Land with the aim of seizing Jerusalem. This they succeeded in doing in 1099, after a month's siege, largely because the Muslims were so divided. However, over the next 200 years a further six major crusades and several minor ones had very mixed fortunes, and ultimately the Christians were unable to maintain control of Palestine. In 1292 the city of Acre, the last major crusader stronghold, fell to the Muslims.

▲ By the time the First Crusade reached Jersualem, it consisted of only 14,000 men. They managed, however, to capture the city and over the next 40 years to establish the boundaries of four crusader states.

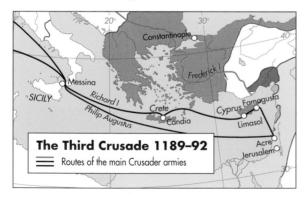

The Third Crusade 1189–92

═	Routes of the main Crusader armies

▲ The arrival of the Third Crusade saved the crusader states from extinction by Saladin, a Kurd who had put an end to the Fatimid Caliphate based in Egypt.

► In the early 12th century the crusaders established the Kingdom of Jerusalem, the County of Tripoli, the Principality of Antioch and the County of Edessa. By 1186 they had lost Edessa.

The Crusader States 1186

	Byzantine Empire
	Cilician Armenia
	Crusader states
	Saladin's territories

→	Amalric's campaigns 1163-69
✕	Battle of Hattin
■	Hospitaller fortress
□	Templar fortress

Battle of Hattin 4th July 1187

▶ Participants in the Fourth Crusade of 1198–1204 were all from Latin Christian countries in Western Europe. They failed to reach Palestine, instead conquering Constantinople, the capital of the Orthodox Christian world. It was two orders of monastic knights – the Hospitallers of St John and the Knights Templar – who helped to ensure the survival of the crusader states. By the early 13th century the crusader states had reached their greatest extent, although they still covered little more than a coastal strip. The Fifth Crusade, with contingents from Germany, Italy, Austria, Hungary, England and France, came close to success in Egypt before its final defeat in 1221.

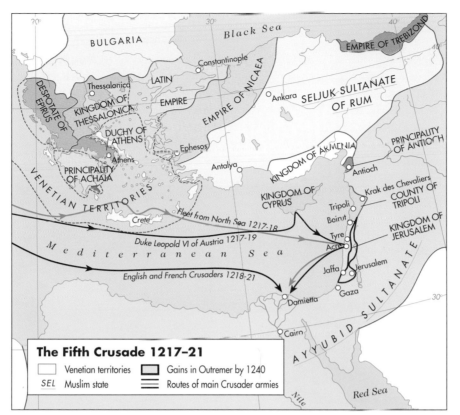

The Fifth Crusade 1217–21

Venetian territories	Gains in Outremer by 1240
SEL Muslim state	Routes of main Crusader armies

▼ In the mid-13th century Islam came under attack from the 'pagan' Mongols, who conquered Central Asia and the area of present-day Iraq and Iran. However, in the same period Islam was permanently established in Anatolia and India, from where it spread to Southeast Asia. Here, Buddhism was the predominant religion, although there were small areas of Hinduism. Despite the influx of Muslims, and the establishment of the Sultanate of Delhi, Hinduism continued to be the main religion in India. Christianity became increasingly identified with Europe, although Christian minorities continued to exist in Egypt, the Middle East and Central Asia.

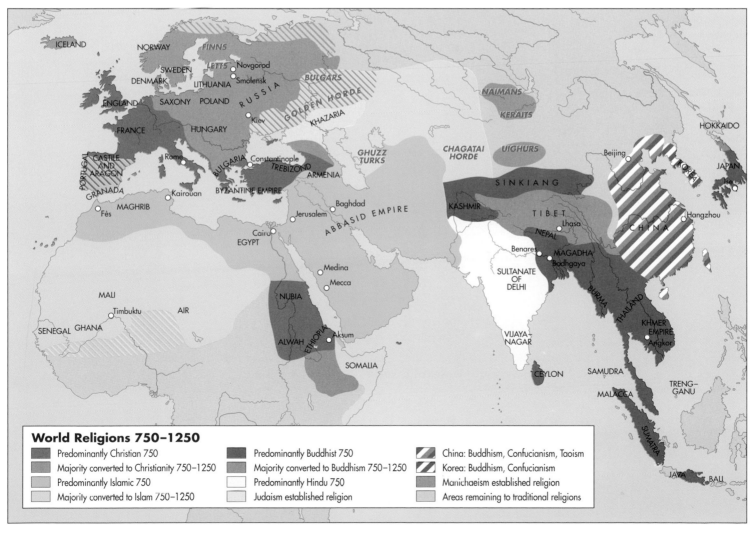

World Religions 750–1250

Predominantly Christian 750	Predominantly Buddhist 750	China: Buddhism, Confucianism, Taoism
Majority converted to Christianity 750–1250	Majority converted to Buddhism 750–1250	Korea: Buddhism, Confucianism
Predominantly Islamic 750	Predominantly Hindu 750	Manichaeism established religion
Majority converted to Islam 750–1250	Judaism established religion	Areas remaining to traditional religions

MEDIEVAL EUROPE

Between 950 and 1300 the population of Europe grew at such a pace that many new villages and towns were established and old towns were developed beyond their existing walls. Urban craftsmen produced an ever-increasing number of goods to sell in the new market-towns and farmers began to produce cash crops such as grain, grapes or wool. Regions started to specialise in, for example, the production of cloth or wine. At the same time, the Genoese and Venetians expanded their territories and gained control of trading routes throughout the Mediterranean Sea. It was via these routes that the Black Death first spread from Asia to Europe, reaching Genoa in January 1348. This pandemic of the bubonic plague went on to devastate most of Europe, resulting in the loss of perhaps a third of its population.

▶ In 1347 the bubonic plague reached the Crimean port of Caffa, from where a fleet of Genoese galleys carried it to Messina and then Genoa. Within four years it had swept through Europe, yet there were towns and regions that remained unaffected.

▶ In medieval Europe the wealth of many regions grew as a result of specialising in the production of particular crops or goods. By the beginning of the 12th century, for example, Flanders was the richest, most densely populated and urbanised region of northern Europe because it had specialised in producing cloth using wool from England. By the 13th century other areas of specialist production included the wine trade of Gascony, grain in Sicily, southern Italy and eastern Europe, timber and fish in Scandinavia and the Baltic, metal-working in the Rhineland, and cheese in eastern England, Holland and southern Poland.

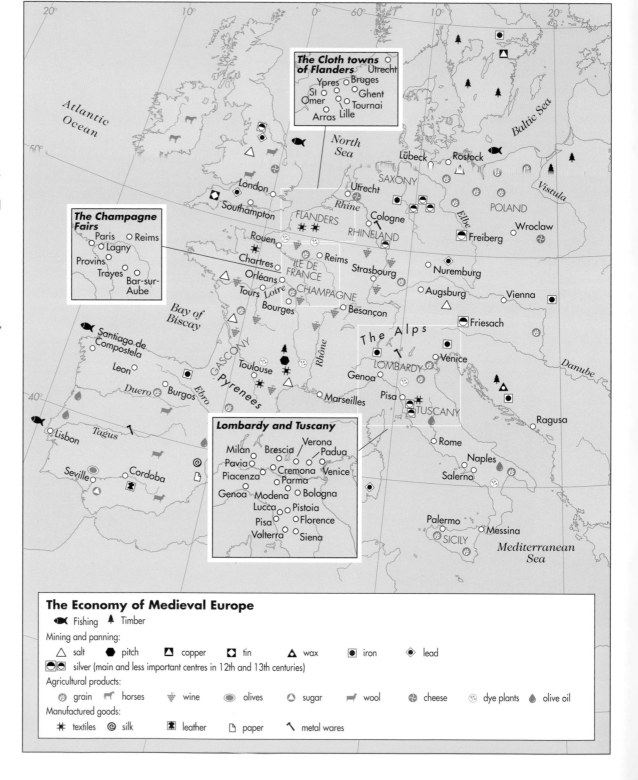

The Cloth towns of Flanders
Utrecht · Ypres · Bruges · Ghent · St Omer · Tournai · Arras · Lille

The Champagne Fairs
Paris · Reims · Lagny · Provins · Troyes · Bar-sur-Aube

Lombardy and Tuscany
Milan · Brescia · Verona · Padua · Pavia · Cremona · Venice · Piacenza · Parma · Genoa · Modena · Bologna · Lucca · Pistoia · Pisa · Florence · Volterra · Siena

The Economy of Medieval Europe

🐟 Fishing   🌲 Timber

Mining and panning:

△ salt   ⬢ pitch   ◩ copper   ◈ tin   ▲ wax   ⊡ iron   ◈ lead

⬚⬚ silver (main and less important centres in 12th and 13th centuries)

Agricultural products:

🌀 grain   🐎 horses   🍇 wine   ⊙ olives   ⌂ sugar   🐑 wool   ⬤ cheese   ◍ dye plants   💧 olive oil

Manufactured goods:

✳ textiles   @ silk   ▣ leather   ▯ paper   🔨 metal wares

The Spread of the Black Death in Europe

Approximate extent of area reached by Black Death in:

1347
1348
1349
1350
1351
1352

Area about which there is insufficient information

Area not affected by Black Death

Town known to have been partly or totally spared by Black Death

Major town very seriously affected by Black Death

Major sea trade route

Novgorod
Reval
Riga
Stockholm
Königsberg
Danzig
Stettin
Lübeck
Hamburg
Bremen
Amsterdam
Antwerp
Liège
Cologne
Frankfurt
Nuremburg
Leipzig
Prague
Vienna
Budapest
Innsbruck
Verona
Venice
Milan
Genoa
Pisa
Florence
Siena
Rome
Naples
Messina
Sicily
Avignon
Arles
Barcelona
Lyon
Geneva
Dijon
Rheims
Paris
Amiens
Rouen
Bordeaux
Madrid
Cordoba
Seville
Cádiz
Lisbon
London
Oxford
Bristol
Leicester
York
Norwich
Edinburgh
Dublin
Kiev
Cracow
Monocastro
Kilia
Varna
Constantinople
Caffa

North Sea
Baltic Sea
Mediterranean Sea
Adriatic Sea
Aegean Sea
Black Sea
Bay of Biscay
The Alps
Carpathians
Pyrenees
Corsica
Sardinia
Crete
Cyprus

Dnieper
Drina
Dvina
Vistula
Elbe
Rhine
Seine
Loire
Rhône
Po
Ebro
Tagus
Dniester
Danube

1347
1348
1349
1350
1351
1352

13

MEDIEVAL BRITAIN

On Christmas Day 1066 William of Normandy was crowned King of England after defeating the English King Harold in the Battle of Hastings. The following year he set about establishing control over his Anglo-Saxon subjects, ruthlessly suppressing any signs of revolt. The lands of the English nobility were distributed among the Norman barons, thus hastening the disappearance of the Anglo-Saxon way of life. In its place, Norman institutions and culture flourished, with Norman French becoming the language of the courts and society. Under a succession of Norman kings, England's prosperity grew and the number of towns rose rapidly. In the countryside a system of feudalism developed, under which each man received land, or the right to work land, in return for services provided to his lord. However, in the second half of the 14th century there were already signs – such as the Peasants' Revolt of 1381 – that the end of feudalism was fast approaching.

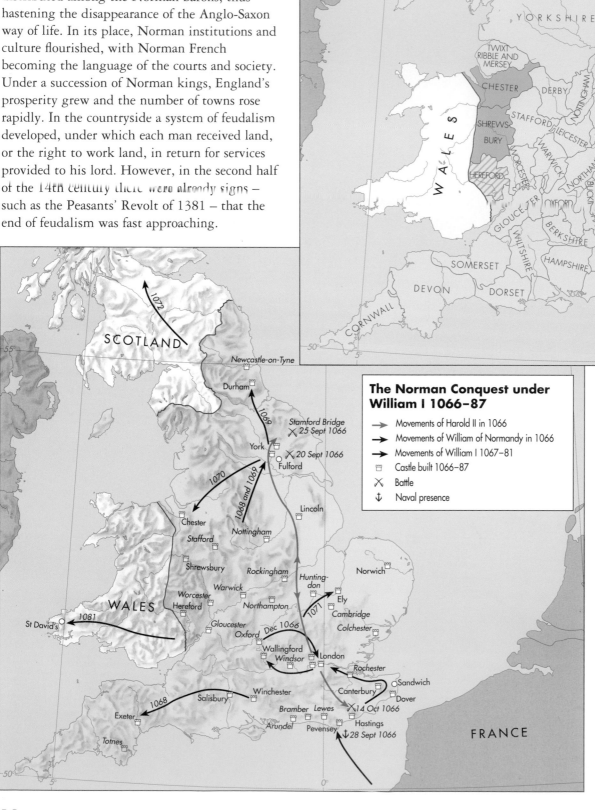

England in 1086
— Shire boundary
▨ Marcher (border) earldom
▨ Former marcher (border) earldom

The Norman Conquest under William I 1066–87
→ Movements of Harold II in 1066
→ Movements of William of Normandy in 1066
→ Movements of William I 1067–81
⌂ Castle built 1066–87
✕ Battle
⬇ Naval presence

◄ In mid-September 1066 King Harold of England marched north to confront an army led by his brother Tostig and Harold Hardrada of Norway. He won a resounding victory at the Battle of Stamford Bridge but then had to march south to fight William of Normandy, who had landed at Pevensey on 28 September. By the time Harold's army reached the coast it was exhausted, thus helping to ensure a Norman victory in the Battle of Hastings on 14 October. After the battle William marched swiftly to London where he was crowned king. From 1067 he dealt swiftly with any signs of opposition from the English and built castles throughout the land to establish Norman control.

In 1086, the year in which the Domesday Survey was completed, England consisted of a pattern of shires which was to last, with only minor changes, until 1974. On the Welsh and Scottish borders there were 'marcher earldoms' which William had created as a means of defending the frontier areas. For the Domesday Survey, information was collected in each shire about the chief towns, the lands of the king and lands of the tenants-in-chief. It showed that since 1066, 1500 foreigners had received lands from the king, and English landholders had almost disappeared.

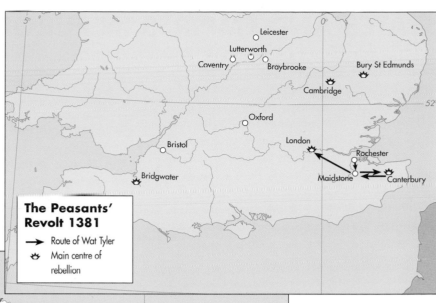

The Peasants' Revolt 1381

→ Route of Wat Tyler

✿ Main centre of rebellion

England, Wales and Scotland in 1400

🏰 Castle

⊗ Fair

○ Cinque port

— Border between English shires and Wales

— Border of Principality of Wales

▲ The Peasants' Revolt of 1381 was mainly a revolt of farmers and tradesmen, with a following of farm labourers, who were angry over the imposition of a very high poll tax. It began in a village in Essex when a tax-collector was killed, and spread quickly to other villages and towns in the southeast. However, the revolt only became a serious threat when a large band of men from Essex and Kent marched to London under the leadership of Wat Tyler. They secured a promise from the king that their demands would be met, but after Tyler was killed by the Mayor of London, the revolt collapsed.

◀ At the end of the 14th century there were stone castles in every part of the country, many built by the Norman kings as a means of establishing their authority. Some were in the middle of flourishing towns, where an enormous variety of crafts and trades were practised. Several towns were also the sites of great fairs. These were held each year and often attracted merchants from as far afield as Flanders, Spain and Germany. A growing volume of trade with these countries was handled by the ports on the south and east coasts.

STATES AND EMPIRES IN EUROPE c.1500–1750

In the 16th century none of the states or empires in mainland Europe were ruled by strong central governments. All were made up of territories that were controlled more by local princes or nobles than by a king or emperor. The ruling dynasties, such as the Habsburgs of Spain and Austria, frequently went to war to establish their claim to various lands. There was also constant warfare in the 17th century, but after 1660 there was a move towards centralisation, most notably in France under King Louis XIV.

▼ From the 15th century the empire established by the Ottoman Turks was one of the most militarily effective states of all time, and in the Christian world its sultan was regarded with great respect. Its decline began in 1683 when a Turkish army laying siege to Vienna was destroyed. However, in the 18th century it was still the largest empire in Europe and western Asia.

The Growth of the Ottoman Empire to 1683

- Ottoman lands 1307
- Ottoman conquests 1307–1481
- Conquests of Selim I 1512–20
- Conquests of Suleiman the Magnificent 1520–66
- Ottoman conquests 1566–1683
- Dependent states
- --- Boundary of Ottoman Empire in 1683
- ✕ Battle, with date

The Growth of the Russian Empire

- Russian territory 1462
- Acquisitions 1462–1533
- Acquisitions 1533–1598
- Acquisitions 1598–1619
- Acquisitions 1619–1689
- Occupied by Russia 1644–89
- Acquisitions 1689–1796
- ⊡ Trading post/fortress (ostrog), with date of foundation
- *SAM* Native people

▼ In the mid-15th century the Russian state of Muscovy was one of many small states in northern Europe that paid tribute to the Tatars. By the end of the 18th century it was at the heart of an immense land empire that stretched from the Baltic in the west, across Siberia, to the Bering Strait in the east.

► Frontiers changed considerably between 1500 and 1560. In 1500, for example, the Habsburgs were just one of a number of ancient dynasties. By the 1520s they had accumulated under Emperor Charles V the largest conglomeration of territories in Europe since the 9th century.

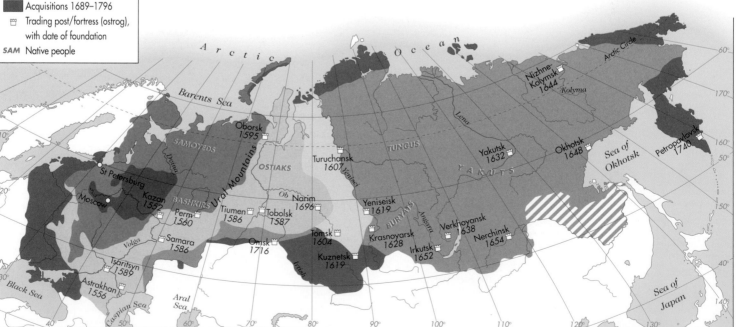

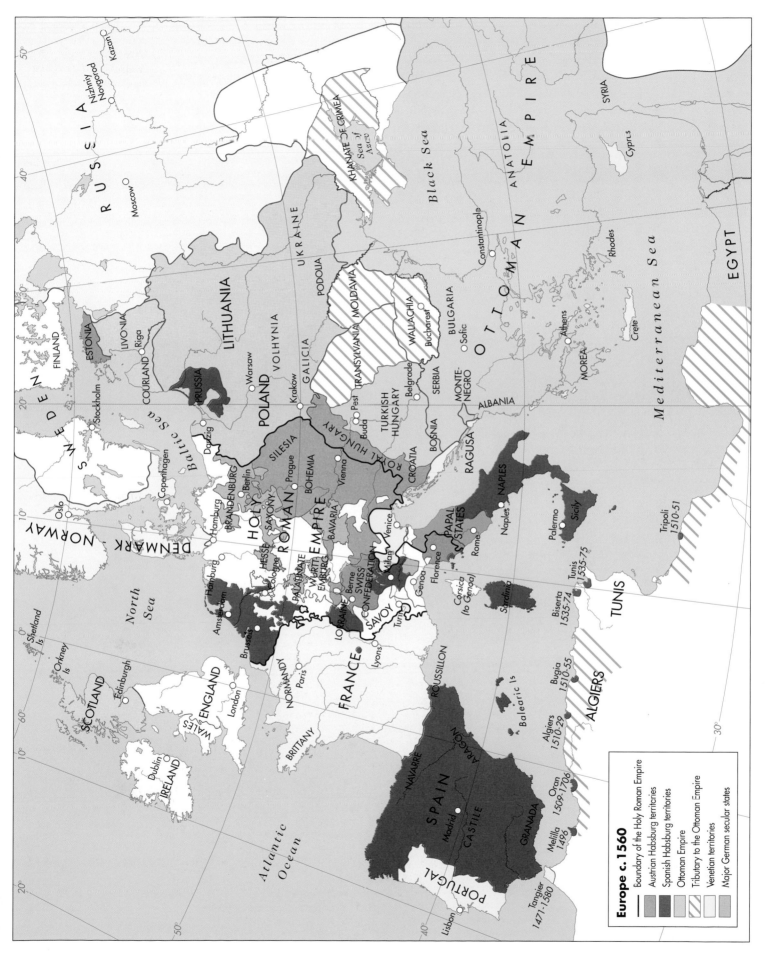

Europe c.1560

- Boundary of the Holy Roman Empire
- Austrian Habsburg territories
- Spanish Habsburg territories
- Ottoman Empire
- Tributary to the Ottoman Empire
- Venetian territories
- Major German secular states

RUSSIA

Nizhniy Novgorod

Kazan

Moscow

FINLAND

ESTONIA

LIVONIA

Riga

COURLAND

LITHUANIA

PRUSSIA

Warsaw

VOLHYNIA

POLAND

Danzig

Krakow

GALICIA

PODOLIA

UKRAINE

KHANATE OF CRIMEA

Sea of Azov

Black Sea

SYRIA

ANATOLIA

OTTOMAN EMPIRE

Constantinople

Cyprus

Rhodes

EGYPT

Mediterranean Sea

Crete

Athens

MOREA

ALBANIA

MONTE-NEGRO

Sofia

BULGARIA

SERBIA

Bucharest

WALLACHIA

MOLDAVIA

TRANSYLVANIA

Belgrade

BOSNIA

RAGUSA

CROATIA

TURKISH HUNGARY

Pest

Buda

ROYAL HUNGARY

SILESIA

Prague

BOHEMIA

Vienna

MORAVIA

SWEDEN

Stockholm

NORWAY

Oslo

DENMARK

Copenhagen

Baltic Sea

Hamburg

BRANDENBURG

Berlin

SAXONY

HOLY ROMAN EMPIRE

HESSE

Cologne

PALATINATE

WÜRTT-EMBURG

BAVARIA

Munich

Berne

SWISS CONFEDERATION

Milan

Venice

SAVOY

Turin

Genoa

Florence

PAPAL STATES

Rome

NAPLES

Naples

Palermo

Sicily

Tripoli 1510-51

Sardinia

Biserta 1535-74

Tunis 1535-75

TUNIS

Corsica (to Genoa)

Balearic Is

Algiers 1510-29

Bugia 1510-55

ALGIERS

Oran 1509-1706

Melilla 1496

SPAIN

Madrid

CASTILE

ARAGON

NAVARRE

GRANADA

ROUSSILLON

PORTUGAL

Lisbon

Tangier 1471-1580

North Sea

Shetland Is

Orkney Is

SCOTLAND

Edinburgh

ENGLAND

WALES

London

IRELAND

Dublin

Atlantic Ocean

Amsterdam

Hamburg

Brussels

LORRAINE

NORMANDY

Paris

BRITTANY

FRANCE

Lyons

Hamburg

NEW PERSPECTIVES IN 16TH-CENTURY EUROPE

In the second half of the 16th century, Europeans embarked on an era of exploration, during which they discovered a sea route around Africa to India and Southeast Asia, and the existence of the Americas. The first circumnavigation of the globe was achieved in 1519–21, and from this point Europeans began to think of the oceans of the world as one vast area of communication. At the same time, both Church and society were transformed by the Protestant Reformation. Beginning as a response to the Catholic Church's reputation for corruption, it resulted in the establishment of Protestant churches in many countries in Europe.

▼ Lutheran, Zwinglian and Calvinist churches were among those established as a result of the Protestant Reformation. In response, the Catholic Church undertook many internal reforms.

The Protestant and Catholic Reformations

- Area where reformed faith dominant by 1580
- Area where reformed faith growing c.1560–70
- Area where considerable local reformed faith c.1560–70
- Area where some penetration of reform c.1560–70
- Area that remained predominantly Catholic
- Area where Lutheranism adopted, with date
- Area where Zwinglianism or Calvinism adopted, with date
- Area where other Protestant Church established (Anglican, Polish, Bohemian)
- † Catholic mission and reform endeavour, with date

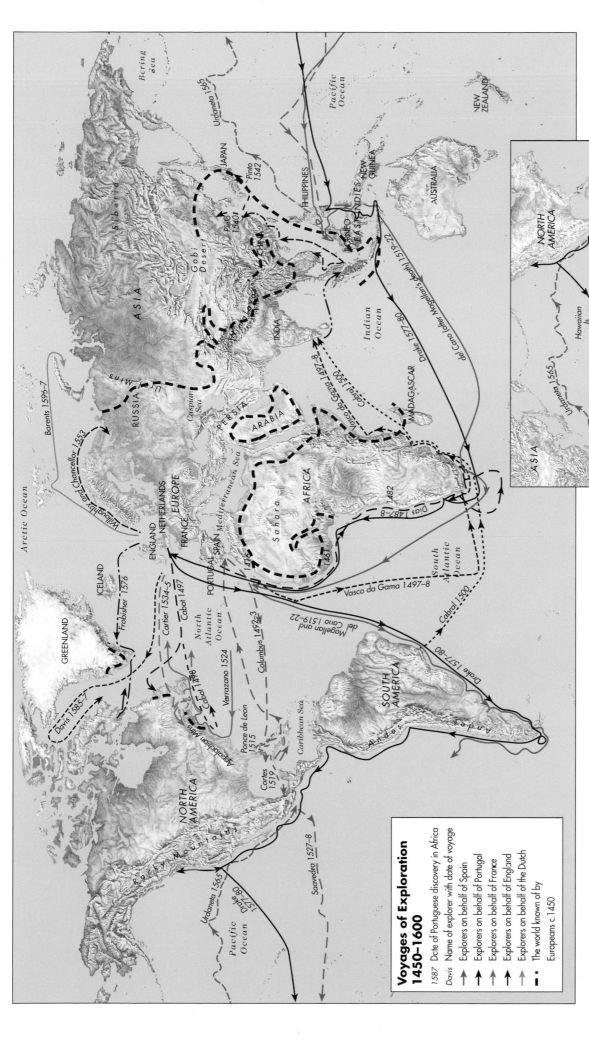

Voyages of Exploration 1450-1600

1587 Date of Portuguese discovery in Africa

Davis Name of explorer with date of voyage

↑ Explorers on behalf of Spain

↑ Explorers on behalf of Portugal

↑ Explorers on behalf of France

↑ Explorers on behalf of England

↑ Explorers on behalf of the Dutch

⋮ The world known of by Europeans c.1450

Routes Across the Pacific

↑ Explorers on behalf of Spain

↑ Explorers on behalf of England

▲ Portuguese explorers led the way in searching for a sea route to the Spice Islands in the east, travelling down the coast of West Africa between 1415 and 1460. In 1488 Dias reached the Cape of Good Hope and in 1497–98 da Gama reached India. Meanwhile, the Spaniards searched in a westerly direction. The result was that between 1492 and 1502 the West Indies and Venezuelan coast were discovered by Columbus. The Spaniards went on to pioneer the route across the Pacific while the British and French explored the coast of North America.

19

TUDOR BRITAIN

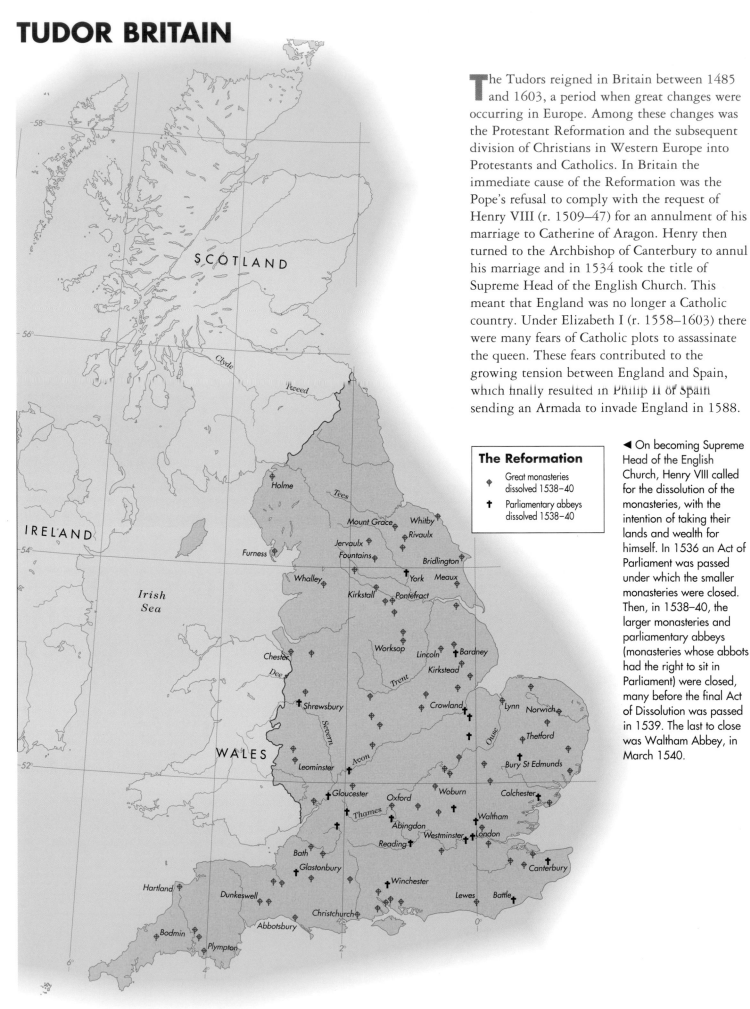

The Tudors reigned in Britain between 1485 and 1603, a period when great changes were occurring in Europe. Among these changes was the Protestant Reformation and the subsequent division of Christians in Western Europe into Protestants and Catholics. In Britain the immediate cause of the Reformation was the Pope's refusal to comply with the request of Henry VIII (r. 1509–47) for an annulment of his marriage to Catherine of Aragon. Henry then turned to the Archbishop of Canterbury to annul his marriage and in 1534 took the title of Supreme Head of the English Church. This meant that England was no longer a Catholic country. Under Elizabeth I (r. 1558–1603) there were many fears of Catholic plots to assassinate the queen. These fears contributed to the growing tension between England and Spain, which finally resulted in Philip II of Spain sending an Armada to invade England in 1588.

The Reformation

✦ Great monasteries dissolved 1538–40

✝ Parliamentary abbeys dissolved 1538–40

◄ On becoming Supreme Head of the English Church, Henry VIII called for the dissolution of the monasteries, with the intention of taking their lands and wealth for himself. In 1536 an Act of Parliament was passed under which the smaller monasteries were closed. Then, in 1538–40, the larger monasteries and parliamentary abbeys (monasteries whose abbots had the right to sit in Parliament) were closed, many before the final Act of Dissolution was passed in 1539. The last to close was Waltham Abbey, in March 1540.

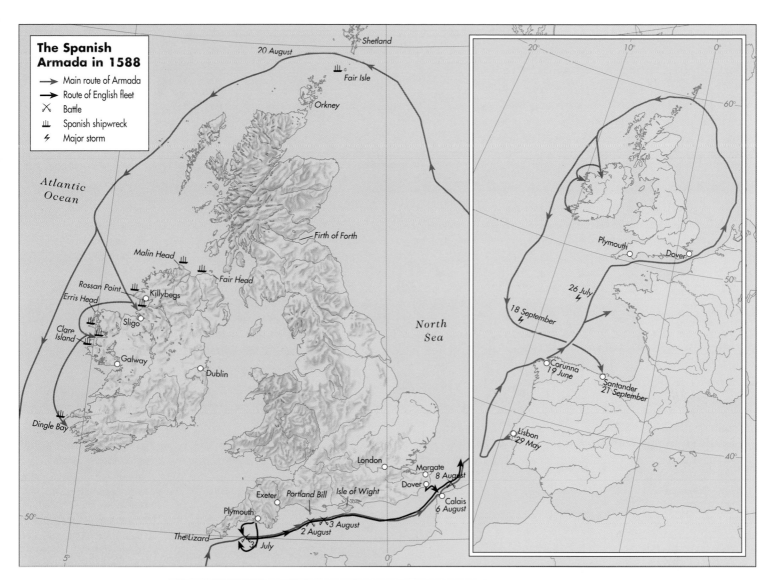

The Spanish Armada in 1588

→ Main route of Armada
→ Route of English fleet
✕ Battle
⚓ Spanish shipwreck
⚡ Major storm

Shetland

20 August

Fair Isle

Orkney

Atlantic Ocean

Firth of Forth

Malin Head

Rossan Point
Erris Head
Fair Head

Killybegs

Clare Island
Sligo

North Sea

Galway

Dublin

Dingle Bay

London
Margate
8 August
Dover
Exeter   *Portland Bill*   *Isle of Wight*   Calais
Plymouth   6 August
The Lizard   3 August
31 July   2 August

20°   10°   0°

60°

Plymouth   Dover

26 July

18 September

50°

Corunna
19 June
Santander
21 September

Lisbon
29 May

40°

5°   0°

▲ The Spanish Armada, consisting of 130 ships, set sail from Lisbon in May 1588, but did not arrive in the English Channel until July. It had a number of minor battles with English ships before reaching Calais, where the intention was to pick up an army of 17,000 men. The English sent fireships into the port, and in the resulting chaos many Spanish ships were destroyed by their opponents' gunnery. The Spaniards then turned north and were pursued as far as the Firth of Forth. They subsequently ran into more storms, and when they finally returned home in September more than half their ships were missing.

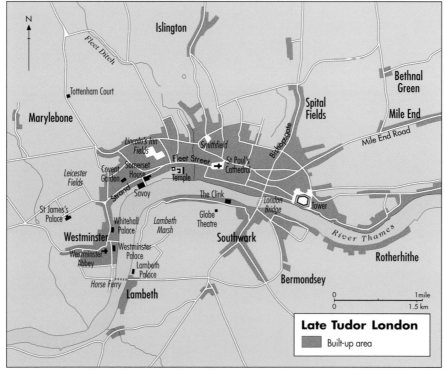

N

Islington

Fleet Ditch

Tottenham Court

Marylebone

Bethnal Green

Spital Fields

Mile End

Mile End Road

Lincoln's Inn Fields   Smithfield
Fleet Street   St Paul's   Bishopsgate
Leicester Fields   Covent Garden   Somerset House   Cathedral
Temple
Strand   Savoy   The Clink   London Bridge   Tower
St James's Palace
Whitehall Palace   Lambeth Marsh   Globe Theatre   Southwark
Westminster   Rotherhithe
Westminster Palace
Westminster Abbey   Lambeth Palace   *River Thames*
Horse Ferry   Bermondsey
Lambeth

0   1 mile
0   1.5 km

Late Tudor London
▆ Built-up area

◄ The population of London grew from about 120,000 in 1550 to almost 200,000 in 1600. Most of these extra people lived in wooden and unsanitary housing that was built to the east of the Tower of London, in suburbs such as Whitechapel and Stepney. To the west, in an almost continuous line that ran along the north side of the Thames for over a mile, there were many splendid palaces surrounded by large gardens. On the south side of the river there were far fewer buildings, but it was here that the first theatre was opened in 1577. The Globe Theatre, at which Shakespeare's plays were performed, was opened in 1599.

BRITAIN 1600–1750

In 1603 King James VI of Scotland became King James I of England, although the two kingdoms were not to be united until 1707. Thus began the reign of the Stuart dynasty uder which James's son, Charles I, was to become extremely unpopular. In 1640 Charles was forced to agree to a set of reforms that gave Parliament more power. These, however, were not considered by some people to be enough and in 1641 Parliament split into two groups – the Royalists (Cavaliers), who supported the King, and the Parliamentarians (Roundheads). The civil war that broke out between the two parties in 1642 was won by the Roundheads in 1646. A second civil war in 1648 led to the execution of Charles I in 1649 and the rise to political power of Oliver Cromwell. A skilled military leader, he was also ruthless in his determination to suppress any opposition, as his campaign in Ireland in 1649–53 demonstrated. His death was followed in 1660 by the restoration of the monarchy and the reigns of King Charles II and King James II.

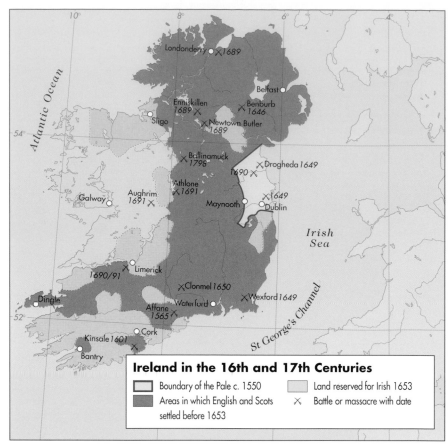

Ireland in the 16th and 17th Centuries

☐ Boundary of the Pale c. 1550	Land reserved for Irish 1653
Areas in which English and Scots settled before 1653	✕ Battle or massacre with date

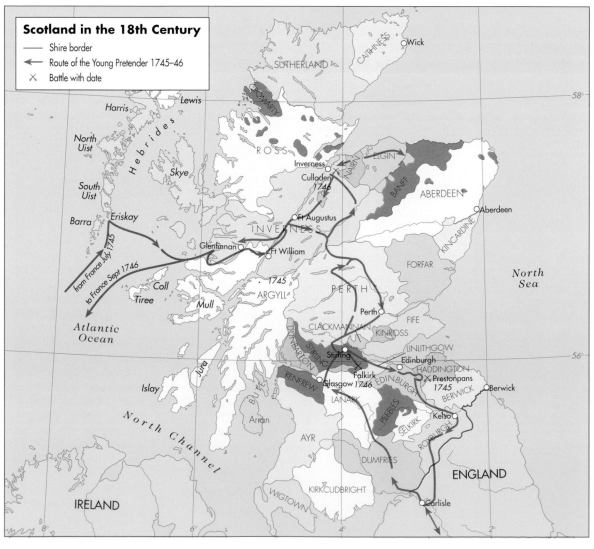

Scotland in the 18th Century

—— Shire border
⟵ Route of the Young Pretender 1745–46
✕ Battle with date

▲ English authority in Ireland was largely confined to a small area around Dublin, known as the Pale, until the late 15th century, when Henry VII began the settlement of the country by Englishmen. In 1653 Cromwell granted a comparatively small area of the country to Irish proprietors who had been loyal to Parliament.

▶ Throughout the English Civil War of 1642–46, the Parliamentarians kept control of London and the southeast while the Royalists were strongest in the north and west. The King used Oxford as his capital.

◀ In 1745 Prince Charles landed in Scotland with the aim of raising support for his campaign to win back the throne of England and Scotland for the Stuarts. His father, King James II, had been deposed in1688. Charles's campaign ended in disaster when his army of Scottish highlanders was defeated at the Battle of Culloden in April 1746.

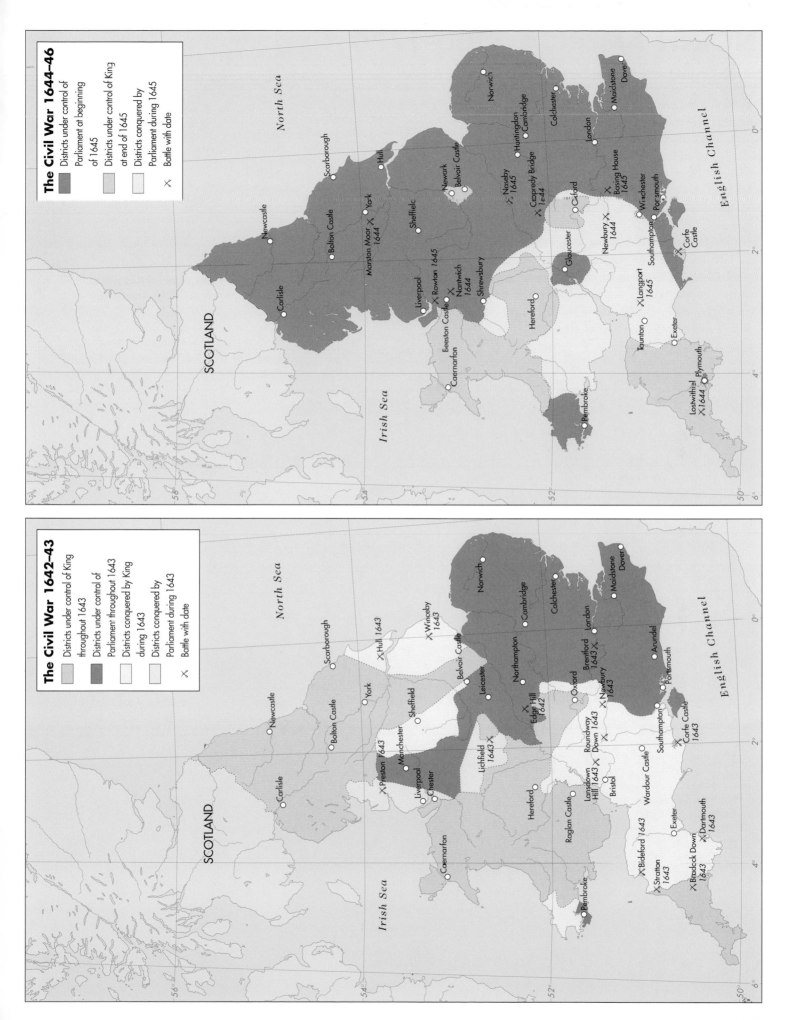

The Civil War 1644-46

Districts under control of Parliament at beginning of 1645

Districts under control of King at end of 1645

Districts conquered by Parliament during 1645

× Battle with date

North Sea

English Channel

SCOTLAND

Newcastle

Carlisle

Scarborough

Hull

Bolton Castle

York

Marston Moor × 1644

Sheffield

Liverpool

× Rowton 1645

× Nantwich 1644

Beeston Castle

Shrewsbury

Caernarfon

Hereford

Pembroke

Newark

Belvoir Castle

× Naseby 1645

× Copredy Bridge 1644

Oxford

Gloucester

Norwich

Huntingdon

Cambridge

Colchester

London

Maidstone

Dover

Basing House 1645 ×

× Newbury 1644

Winchester

Southampton

Portsmouth

× Corfe Castle

Taunton

× Langport 1645

Exeter

Lostwithiel × 1644

Plymouth

Irish Sea

The Civil War 1642-43

Districts under control of King throughout 1643

Districts under control of Parliament throughout 1643

Districts conquered by King during 1643

Districts conquered by Parliament during 1643

× Battle with date

North Sea

English Channel

SCOTLAND

Newcastle

Carlisle

Scarborough

Bolton Castle

York

× Hull 1643

× Winceby 1643

Belvoir Castle

Sheffield

× Preston 1643

Manchester

Liverpool

Chester

× Lichfield 1643 ×

Leicester

Northampton

× Edge Hill 1642

Oxford

× Brentford 1643 ×

× Newbury 1643

Norwich

Cambridge

Colchester

London

Maidstone

Dover

Arundel

Portsmouth

× Southampton

Corfe Castle 1643 ×

Hereford

Raglan Castle

Caernarfon

Pembroke

× Roundway Down 1643 ×

× Lansdown Hill 1643

Bristol

Wardour Castle

× Bideford 1643

Exeter

× Dartmouth 1643

× Stratton 1643

× Braddock Down 1643

Irish Sea

NORTH AMERICA 1500–1770

When Europeans arrived on the shores of North America in the 16th century, many different ways of life existed among the native inhabitants. Farming communities were established in large areas of the south, and in the southeast there were towns of up to 30,000 inhabitants. Elsewhere, people's livelihood depended to a varying extent on hunting, fishing, gathering, agriculture and trade. The Europeans attempted to found colonies, but none survived until the following century, when Britain, France, Spain and Holland created major empires on the mainland and in the Caribbean. Some Native Americans responded to the arrival of the Europeans by moving west. In the northeast a number of previously warring groups settled their differences and became involved in the wars between the rival European powers.

► Some Native American peoples had a nomadic way of life before the arrival of the Europeans. After the introduction of the horse by the Spaniards in the 16th century, they were able to travel great distances more easily.

▼ The horse revolutionised hunting techniques, enabling the regular and efficient slaughter of animals. In the 16th and 17th centuries many Plains tribes abandoned their traditional way of life, and adopted one based on horseback hunting, mainly of buffalo.

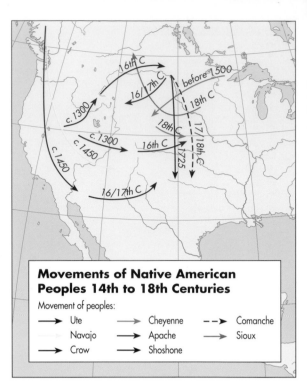

Movements of Native American Peoples 14th to 18th Centuries

Movement of peoples:

→ Ute	→ Cheyenne	--→ Comanche
Navajo	→ Apache	→ Sioux
→ Crow	→ Shoshone	

Native American Peoples c.1500

Cultural area:

- California
- Plateau
- Northwest Coast
- Arctic
- Subarctic
- Great Plains
- Great Basin
- Southwest
- Eastern Woodlands
- *CRO* Native American people c.1500

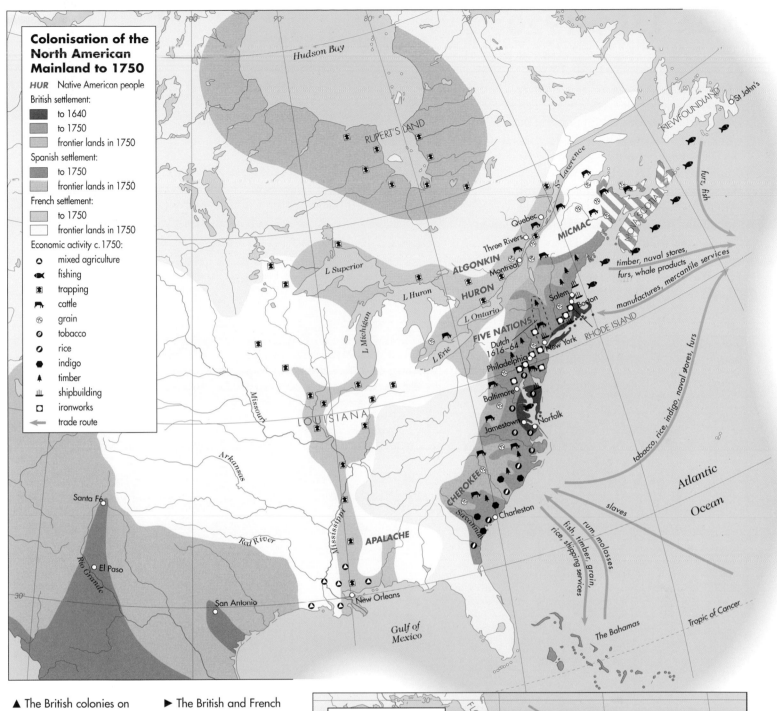

Colonisation of the North American Mainland to 1750

HUR Native American people

British settlement:
- to 1640
- to 1750
- frontier lands in 1750

Spanish settlement:
- to 1750
- frontier lands in 1750

French settlement:
- to 1750
- frontier lands in 1750

Economic activity c. 1750:
- mixed agriculture
- fishing
- trapping
- cattle
- grain
- tobacco
- rice
- indigo
- timber
- shipbuilding
- ironworks
- trade route

▲ The British colonies on the mainland were set up in two main waves: from 1603 to 1634, when settlements were established in Virginia, Maryland and New England, and from 1664 to 1680, when the Carolinas and Pennsylvania were founded and New York was seized from the Dutch. In the early 17th century the French established fishing and trading colonies in Canada. Later, they colonised the area around the Mississippi, but by 1763 this was lost to the British and Spaniards.

▶ The British and French colonies in the Caribbean had an environment in which disease flourished. Consequently, in the early years the majority of immigrants to these colonies were white bondsmen, who provided several years of unpaid labour – usually on tobacco plantations – in exchange for the cost of their passage and a plot of free land. Around 1640 a shift from tobacco to sugar production increased the demand for labour and slaves began to be imported from Africa.

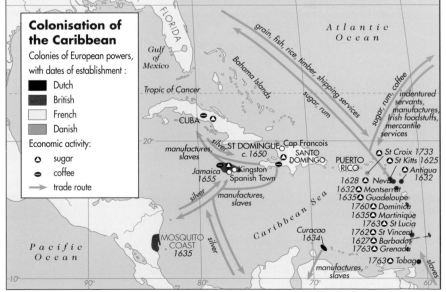

Colonisation of the Caribbean

Colonies of European powers, with dates of establishment :
- Dutch
- British
- French
- Danish

Economic activity:
- sugar
- coffee
- trade route

ASIA 1500–1920

In the 16th century the Mughal Empire in India and the Ming Empire in China were two of the greatest powers in the world. By the end of the 18th century the Mughal Empire had only symbolic significance, and real power was in the hands of numerous princes and of the British. In China the Ming Dynasty had been replaced by the Manchus, and there was a growing threat from European powers who were eager to trade freely throughout Asia. When, in 1842, Britain forced the Manchus to lift the ban on the opium trade and open ports to European merchants, it was clear that China was no longer a world power.

Ming and Manchu Qing Imperial Borders

- ■ Area under Ming Dynasty 1600
- ■ Additional area under Manchu Dynasty in 1840
- □ Manchu vassal state

Rebuilding of the Great Wall in:
- —— 14th century
- – – – 15th–16th centuries
- ·········· 16th century

▲ Under the Ming Dynasty of 1368–1644, China's cultural, political and economic strength grew. The European powers presented no real threat, the Chinese navy twice succeeding in defeating Dutch fleets off the south coast in 1622–24. A more serious threat was posed by the nomadic Manchus who lived to the north of the Great Wall. In 1644 they seized control in Beijing and established a dynasty under which the Chinese Empire expanded to its greatest extent ever, encompassing Manchuria, Mongolia, Turkestan and Tibet. From 1800 onwards, the Manchus were increasingly under threat from uprisings caused by famine and a corrupt and inadequately funded government. Aggressive Western powers also played a part in undermining Manchu power, which finally came to an end in 1911 with a revolution that established China as a republic.

▶ The Mughal Empire was founded in 1526 by Babur, the Sultan of Kabul. Under Babur's grandson Akbar (1556–1605), the empire was expanded and centralised. Domestic industries, trade, art and architecture all flourished. Aurangzeb (1658–1707) attempted to expand the empire southwards, but he was unable to deal effectively with his many opponents and the empire went into fast decline.

Mughal India

- □ Approximate extent of Mughal Empire 1605
- ■ Additional area claimed by Mughals 1707
- —— Boundaries of provinces (subahs) 1707
- ● Provincial (subah) headquarters 1707
- ➡ Advance of Marathas
- **MA** People in rebellion against the empire c.1700

Major European trading posts by 1700:
⊠ Portuguese	⊠ British
⊠ Danish	⊠ French
⊠ Dutch	

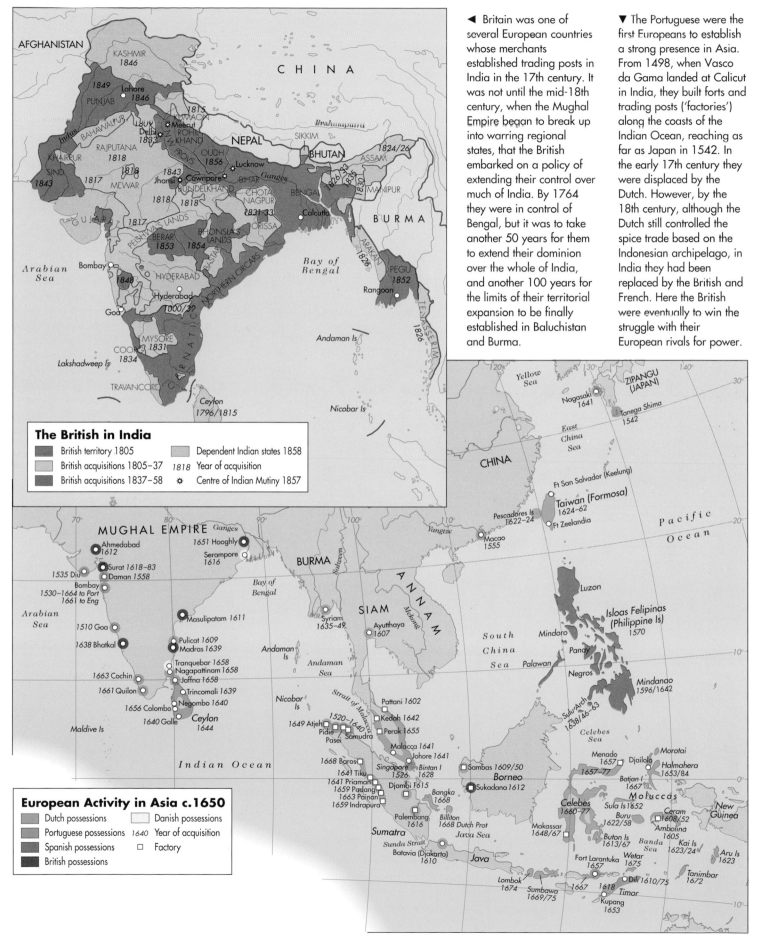

◄ Britain was one of several European countries whose merchants established trading posts in India in the 17th century. It was not until the mid-18th century, when the Mughal Empire began to break up into warring regional states, that the British embarked on a policy of extending their control over much of India. By 1764 they were in control of Bengal, but it was to take another 50 years for them to extend their dominion over the whole of India, and another 100 years for the limits of their territorial expansion to be finally established in Baluchistan and Burma.

▼ The Portuguese were the first Europeans to establish a strong presence in Asia. From 1498, when Vasco da Gama landed at Calicut in India, they built forts and trading posts ('factories') along the coasts of the Indian Ocean, reaching as far as Japan in 1542. In the early 17th century they were displaced by the Dutch. However, by the 18th century, although the Dutch still controlled the spice trade based on the Indonesian archipelago, in India they had been replaced by the British and French. Here the British were eventually to win the struggle with their European rivals for power.

The British in India

- British territory 1805
- British acquisitions 1805–37
- British acquisitions 1837–58
- Dependent Indian states 1858
- *1818* Year of acquisition
- ✸ Centre of Indian Mutiny 1857

European Activity in Asia c.1650

- Dutch possessions
- Portuguese possessions
- Spanish possessions
- British possessions
- Danish possessions
- *1640* Year of acquisition
- □ Factory

REVOLUTIONARY AND NAPOLEONIC EUROPE

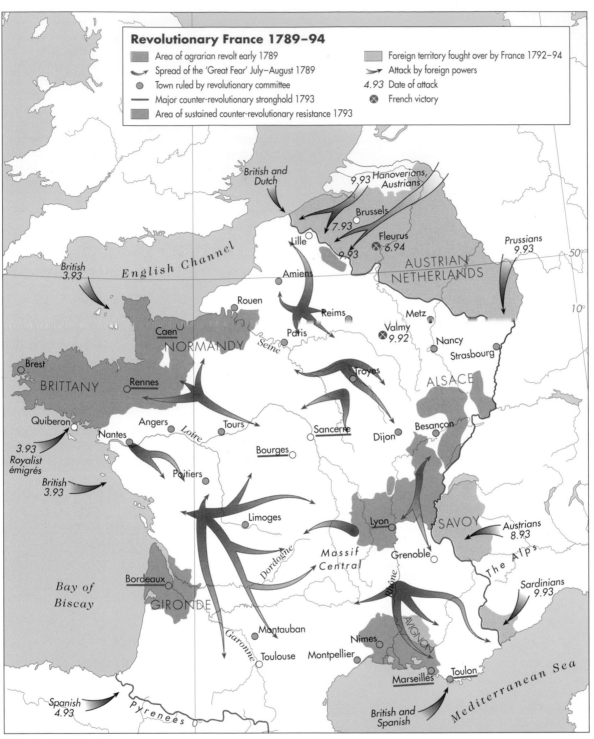

Revolutionary France 1789–94

- Area of agrarian revolt early 1789
- Spread of the 'Great Fear' July–August 1789
- Town ruled by revolutionary committee
- Major counter-revolutionary stronghold 1793
- Area of sustained counter-revolutionary resistance 1793
- Foreign territory fought over by France 1792–94
- Attack by foreign powers
- 4.93 Date of attack
- French victory

British and Dutch

English Channel

British 3.93

Hanoverians, Austrians 9.93

Brussels

7.93

Fleurus 6.94

9.93

AUSTRIAN NETHERLANDS

Prussians 9.93

Lille

Amiens

Rouen

Reims

Metz

Paris

Valmy 9.92

Nancy

Strasbourg

Caen

NORMANDY

Seine

ALSACE

Troyes

Brest

BRITTANY

Rennes

Angers

Loire

Tours

Sancerre

Dijon

Besançon

Quiberon

3.93 Royalist émigrés

Nantes

Bourges

Poitiers

British 3.93

Limoges

Dordogne

Massif Central

Lyon

SAVOY

Austrians 8.93

Grenoble

The Alps

Sardinians 9.93

Bay of Biscay

Bordeaux

GIRONDE

Garonne

Montauban

Toulouse

Nimes

Montpellier

AVIGNON

Rhône

Marseilles

Toulon

British and Spanish

Mediterranean Sea

Spanish 4.93

Pyrenees

◄ Early in 1789, following a poor harvest, peasants and industrial labourers in parts of France rioted. In Paris, meanwhile, the king had been forced to call a meeting of the Estates-General (parliament) in order to raise extra taxes. The representatives of the middle-classes (the 'Third Estate') took this opportunity to reject co-operation with the other two Estates (aristocracy and clergy) and declare themselves a National Assembly. Riots in Paris on 14 July 1789 spread throughout France, stirred up by revolutionary committees. Peasants looted and destroyed the property of the aristocracy in what became known as the 'Great Fear'. Foreign monarchs sent armies in an attempt to aid the French king, but this only hastened his execution, which took place in January 1793. During 1793 and 1794 France successfully defended itself against foreign invaders on all sides, and counter-revolutionary uprisings in the west and south.

The French Revolution began in July 1789 when the middle classes seized power at the same time as peasants and industrial workers were driven by poverty and starvation to riot against the property-owning aristocracy. Anti-monarchist feeling led to the execution of King Louis XIV in January 1793. A reign of terror ensued, during which 40,000 people were executed, when extremists, led by Robespierre, sought to impose the revolution. From mid-1794 a more moderate faction gained power, but this was overthrown in 1799 by Napoleon, who became First Consul of France. He oversaw major reforms of French government, including the drafting of the Napoleonic Civil Code, which became the basis of legal systems in many countries. In 1804 he proclaimed himself Emperor – an act many considered a betrayal of revolutionary principles.

Vitoria 6.1813

Corunna 1.1809

Valladolid 7.1808

Sar 2

Salamanca 7.1812

Somosier 11.1

Vimeiro 8.1808

Talavera 7.1809

Madrid

PORTUGAL

SPAIN

Trafalgar 10.1805

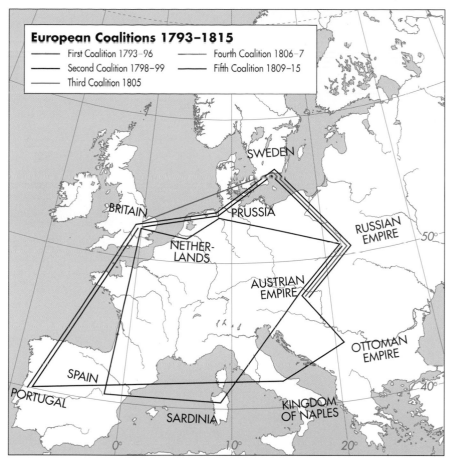

European Coalitions 1793–1815

First Coalition 1793–96	Fourth Coalition 1806–7
Second Coalition 1798–99	Fifth Coalition 1809–15
Third Coalition 1805	

◀ The French Revolution caused concern among the rulers of other European countries. Initially they feared a spread of revolutionary fervour to their own countries; later it became clear that the main threat was of invasion, as Napoleon attempted, by the use of military power, to impose his legal and administrative systems across Europe. Opposition to Napoleon's France brought together the European powers in a succession of coalitions. Britain was a constant member, with other countries joining when it was in their interest to do so. Russia also joined all five coalitions but, following its defeat in 1807, became an ally of France until 1810.

▼ Napoleon rose to fame as a general, with success in Italy in the 1790s. Despite a failed attempt to cut British trade routes in Egypt, he swept to power in 1799. He then embarked on a process of extending French rule across Europe. Spain became a French puppet state until the Spaniards revolted in 1808 and, supported by the Fifth Coalition, fought the Peninsular War. Napoleon's invasion of Russia in 1812 failed, however, when French supply lines were stretched and his troops were forced to retreat. Napoleon was captured in France in 1814, escaped, and was defeated at Waterloo on 18 June 1815.

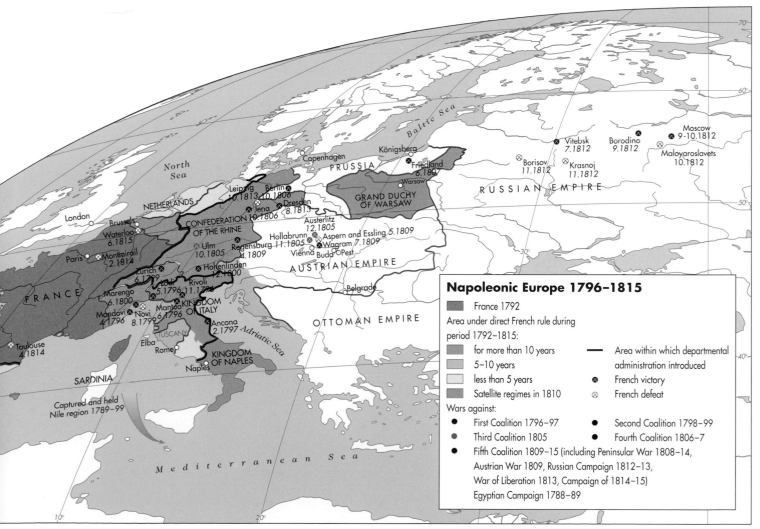

Napoleonic Europe 1796–1815

- France 1792

Area under direct French rule during period 1792–1815:
- for more than 10 years
- 5–10 years
- less than 5 years
- Satellite regimes in 1810

— Area within which departmental administration introduced
- ⊗ French victory
- ⊗ French defeat

Wars against:
- First Coalition 1796–97
- Third Coalition 1805
- Second Coalition 1798–99
- Fourth Coalition 1806–7
- Fifth Coalition 1809–15 (including Peninsular War 1808–14, Austrian War 1809, Russian Campaign 1812–13, War of Liberation 1813, Campaign of 1814–15)
- Egyptian Campaign 1788–89

INDEPENDENCE IN NORTH AMERICA

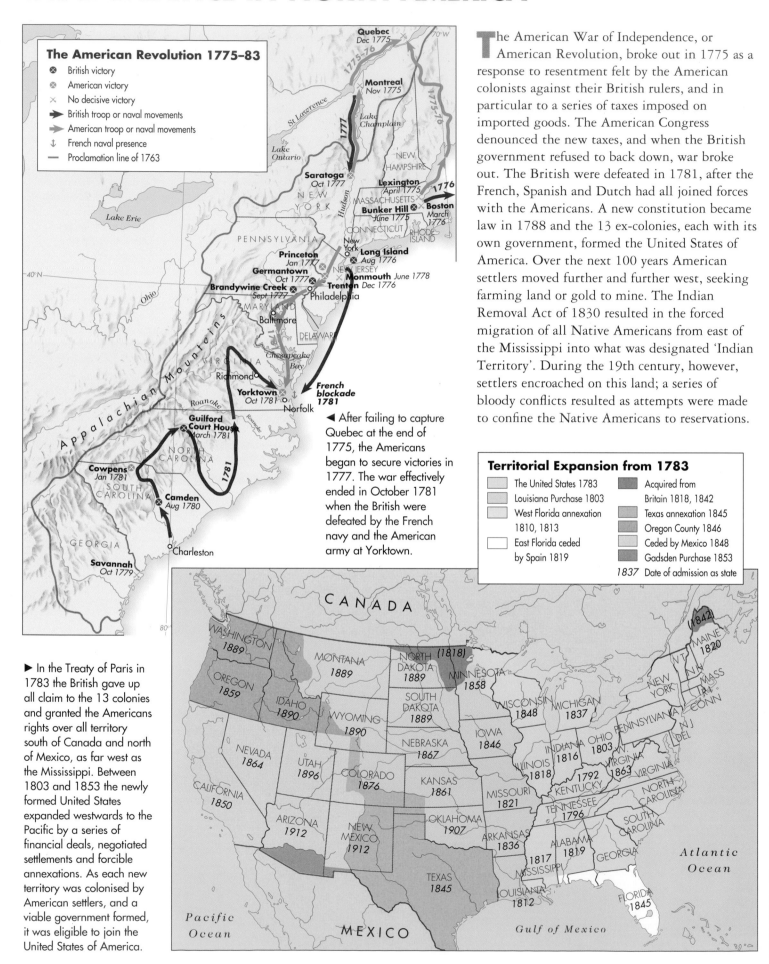

The American Revolution 1775–83

⊗ British victory
⊗ American victory
✕ No decisive victory
➔ British troop or naval movements
➔ American troop or naval movements
↓ French naval presence
— Proclamation line of 1763

Quebec
Dec 1775

1775–76

Montreal
Nov 1775

St Lawrence

Lake
Ontario

Lake
Champlain

1777

Lake Erie

NEW
HAMPSHIRE

Saratoga
Oct 1777

Lexington
April 1775

Bunker Hill
June 1775

Boston
March
1776

1776

N E W
Y O R K

MASSACHUSETTS

CONNECTICUT

RHODE
ISLAND

PENNSYLVANIA

Hudson

New
York

Long Island
Aug 1776

Princeton
Jan 1777

Germantown
Oct 1777

Brandywine Creek
Sept 1777

NEW JERSEY

Monmouth June 1778

Trenton Dec 1776

Philadelphia

Ohio

MARYLAND

Baltimore

DELAWARE

VIRGINIA

Chesapeake
Bay

Richmond

Appalachian Mountains

Roanoke

Yorktown
Oct 1781

French
blockade
1781

Norfolk

Guilford
Court House
March 1781

Roanoke

NORTH
CAROLINA

1781

Cowpens
Jan 1781

SOUTH
CAROLINA

Camden
Aug 1780

GEORGIA

Charleston

Savannah
Oct 1779

◄ After failing to capture Quebec at the end of 1775, the Americans began to secure victories in 1777. The war effectively ended in October 1781 when the British were defeated by the French navy and the American army at Yorktown.

The American War of Independence, or American Revolution, broke out in 1775 as a response to resentment felt by the American colonists against their British rulers, and in particular to a series of taxes imposed on imported goods. The American Congress denounced the new taxes, and when the British government refused to back down, war broke out. The British were defeated in 1781, after the French, Spanish and Dutch had all joined forces with the Americans. A new constitution became law in 1788 and the 13 ex-colonies, each with its own government, formed the United States of America. Over the next 100 years American settlers moved further and further west, seeking farming land or gold to mine. The Indian Removal Act of 1830 resulted in the forced migration of all Native Americans from east of the Mississippi into what was designated 'Indian Territory'. During the 19th century, however, settlers encroached on this land; a series of bloody conflicts resulted as attempts were made to confine the Native Americans to reservations.

Territorial Expansion from 1783

☐ The United States 1783
☐ Louisiana Purchase 1803
☐ West Florida annexation 1810, 1813
☐ East Florida ceded by Spain 1819
☐ Acquired from Britain 1818, 1842
☐ Texas annexation 1845
☐ Oregon County 1846
☐ Ceded by Mexico 1848
☐ Gadsden Purchase 1853
1837 Date of admission as state

► In the Treaty of Paris in 1783 the British gave up all claim to the 13 colonies and granted the Americans rights over all territory south of Canada and north of Mexico, as far west as the Mississippi. Between 1803 and 1853 the newly formed United States expanded westwards to the Pacific by a series of financial deals, negotiated settlements and forcible annexations. As each new territory was colonised by American settlers, and a viable government formed, it was eligible to join the United States of America.

CANADA

WASHINGTON
1889

MONTANA
1889

NORTH
DAKOTA
1889

(1818)

MINNESOTA
1858

(1842)

MAINE
1820

VT
N.H.

OREGON
1859

IDAHO
1890

WYOMING
1890

SOUTH
DAKOTA
1889

WISCONSIN
1848

MICHIGAN
1837

NEW
YORK

MASS

R.I.
CONN

NEVADA
1864

UTAH
1896

COLORADO
1876

NEBRASKA
1867

IOWA
1846

ILLINOIS
1818

INDIANA
1816

OHIO
1803

PENNSYLVANIA

VIRGINIA
1792

VIRGINIA
1863

NJ
DEL

CALIFORNIA
1850

ARIZONA
1912

NEW
MEXICO
1912

KANSAS
1861

MISSOURI
1821

KENTUCKY
1792

TENNESSEE
1796

NORTH
CAROLINA

OKLAHOMA
1907

ARKANSAS
1836

ALABAMA
1819

GEORGIA

SOUTH
CAROLINA

Atlantic
Ocean

TEXAS
1845

MISSISSIPPI
1817

LOUISIANA
1812

FLORIDA
1845

Pacific
Ocean

MEXICO

Gulf of Mexico

Routes of Exploration and Settlement

Routes of:

— Lewis and Clark 1804–6
— Pike 1804–7
— Long 1817–23
— Settlers' trail
- - - Cattle trail
⊡ Mining, with date when it began

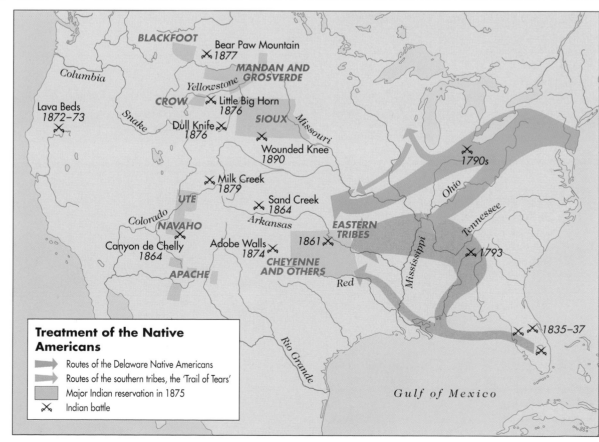

▲ By 1800 the region east of the Mississippi was well explored, as was the west coast of America. By 1806 a government-funded expedition, led by Lewis and Clark, had established a route between the two. Alternative overland routes were established by settlers seeking land or gold. Other routes were used by farmers bringing cattle to the slaughterhouses.

► During the 18th century the Native Americans from Delaware made a slow westward migration and in 1830 the Indian Removal Act forced the southern tribes to move west too. Demands by white settlers for more land led to the Indian reservations and a series of bloody conflicts, as the Native Americans resisted attempts to restrict them to the reservations.

Treatment of the Native Americans

➤ Routes of the Delaware Native Americans
➤ Routes of the southern tribes, the 'Trail of Tears'
▮ Major Indian reservation in 1875
✕ Indian battle

AFRICA AND THE SLAVE TRADE

▼ At the beginning of the 19th century there were few Europeans in Africa outside the coastal regions of the north, west and south. The internal trading network was controlled by independent kingdoms which, as the century progressed, came under threat both from Europeans and from the southward advance of Islam.

After exploring the west coast of Africa between 1420 and 1460, the Portuguese began to trade in slaves, acquiring them in exchange for firearms and manufactured goods, and shipping them across the Atlantic to the Americas. Other European nations quickly became involved in the trade, and between 1450 and 1900 over 12 million slaves were sent to work on plantations producing a variety of crops in North and South America and the Caribbean. However, at the beginning of the 19th century the interior of Africa, with its many independent kingdoms, was still little known to outsiders. It would be another 80 years before the European powers would begin to divide up the continent amongst themselves.

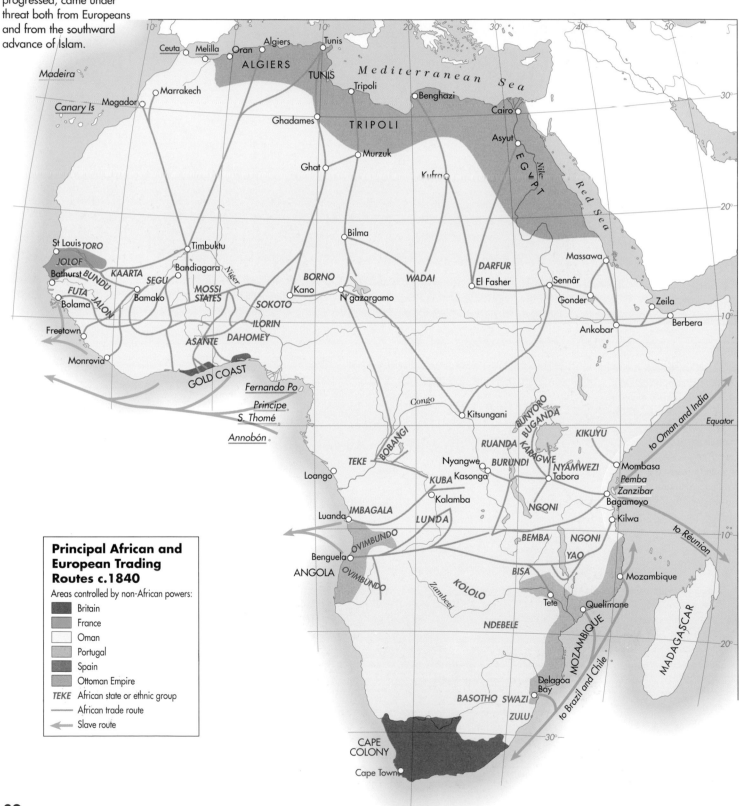

Principal African and European Trading Routes c.1840

Areas controlled by non-African powers:

- Britain
- France
- Oman
- Portugal
- Spain
- Ottoman Empire

TEKE African state or ethnic group

African trade route

Slave route

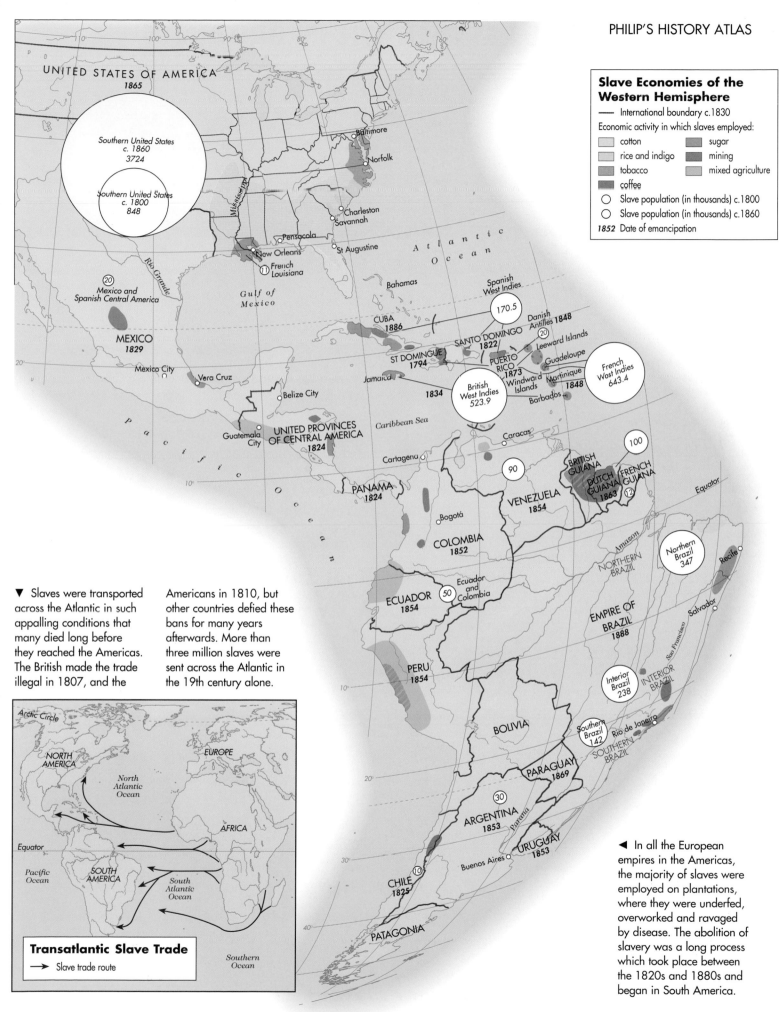

Slave Economies of the Western Hemisphere

—— International boundary c.1830

Economic activity in which slaves employed:

cotton	sugar
rice and indigo	mining
tobacco	mixed agriculture
coffee	

○ Slave population (in thousands) c.1800

◯ Slave population (in thousands) c.1860

1852 Date of emancipation

UNITED STATES OF AMERICA
1865

Southern United States
c. 1860
3724

Southern United States
c. 1800
848

Baltimore

Norfolk

Charleston
Savannah

Pensacola

St Augustine

New Orleans

11 French
Louisiana

*Atlantic
Ocean*

20 Mexico and
Spanish Central America

*Gulf of
Mexico*

Bahamas

Spanish
West Indies

MEXICO
1829

Mexico City

Vera Cruz

CUBA
1886

170.5

Danish
Antilles *1848*

20

SANTO DOMINGO
1822

ST DOMINGUE
1794

Jamaica

1834

PUERTO
RICO
1873

Leeward Islands

Guadeloupe

Windward
Islands
Martinique
1848

Barbados

French
West Indies
643.4

British
West Indies
523.9

Rio Grande

Mississippi

Caribbean Sea

Belize City

UNITED PROVINCES
OF CENTRAL AMERICA
1824

Guatemala
City

PANAMA
1824

Caracas

Cartagena

90

VENEZUELA
1854

BRITISH
GUIANA

DUTCH
GUIANA
1863

FRENCH
GUIANA

12

100

Equator

Bogotá

COLOMBIA
1852

Amazon

NORTHERN
BRAZIL

Northern
Brazil
347

Recife

ECUADOR
1854

50 Ecuador
and
Colombia

EMPIRE OF
BRAZIL
1888

Salvador

São Francisco

PERU
1854

Interior
Brazil
238

INTERIOR
BRAZIL

BOLIVIA

Southern
Brazil
142

Rio de Janeiro

SOUTHERN
BRAZIL

PARAGUAY
1869

30

ARGENTINA
1853

Paraná

URUGUAY
1853

10

Buenos Aires

CHILE
1825

PATAGONIA

▼ Slaves were transported across the Atlantic in such appalling conditions that many died long before they reached the Americas. The British made the trade illegal in 1807, and the Americans in 1810, but other countries defied these bans for many years afterwards. More than three million slaves were sent across the Atlantic in the 19th century alone.

Transatlantic Slave Trade

Arctic Circle

NORTH
AMERICA

EUROPE

*North
Atlantic
Ocean*

AFRICA

Equator

*Pacific
Ocean*

SOUTH
AMERICA

*South
Atlantic
Ocean*

Southern
Ocean

→ Slave trade route

◄ In all the European empires in the Americas, the majority of slaves were employed on plantations, where they were underfed, overworked and ravaged by disease. The abolition of slavery was a long process which took place between the 1820s and 1880s and began in South America.

33

THE INDUSTRIAL REVOLUTION IN BRITAIN

Until the 1750s in Britain, cloth and other goods were manufactured in small, home-based industries. In the second half of the 18th century the invention of machines for spinning thread and for weaving material, and the development of steam engines that could drive this machinery, led to the building of large factories, often employing hundreds of workers. The goods produced by the factories were initially transported by water, but from 1825 onwards a railway network was developed. Britain's population almost trebled from 1750 to 1850, with more than half the people living in towns or cities by the end of the period.

The Cotton Textile Industry 1850

—— Navigable river	▨ Coalfield	⬤ Population of city in '000s for
⊢⊢⊢ Canal	# Cotton factories	1750 (inner) and 1850 (outer)
—— Railway		

Resources and Development in England 1750

▨ Coalfield
—— Navigable river

Industries:
- \# fustian and linen cloth
- ✿ woollen cloth
- ▲ copper mining and smelting
- ⬘ tin mining and smelting
- ▣ iron extraction and smelting
- ✾ metalware and cutlery
- ⊥⊥⊥ shipbuilding

▲ While early factories were powered by waterwheels, and therefore had to be sited next to running water, the development of steam power from the 1780s onwards meant that factories were increasingly sited where they could easily be supplied with coal and raw materials. Large urban centres sprang up, linked by canals and railways. Lancashire, close to coalfields and with a well-established textile industry, became a major industrial region, with a rapidly developing transport network. By the 1830s one-third of its population was employed in the cotton factories and related industries.

◄ In 1750 most people lived in the countryside. Some worked on the land, but many produced cloth and smelted metals in small, home-based industries. London was the largest manufacturing centre, producing silk, gin, soap and glass.

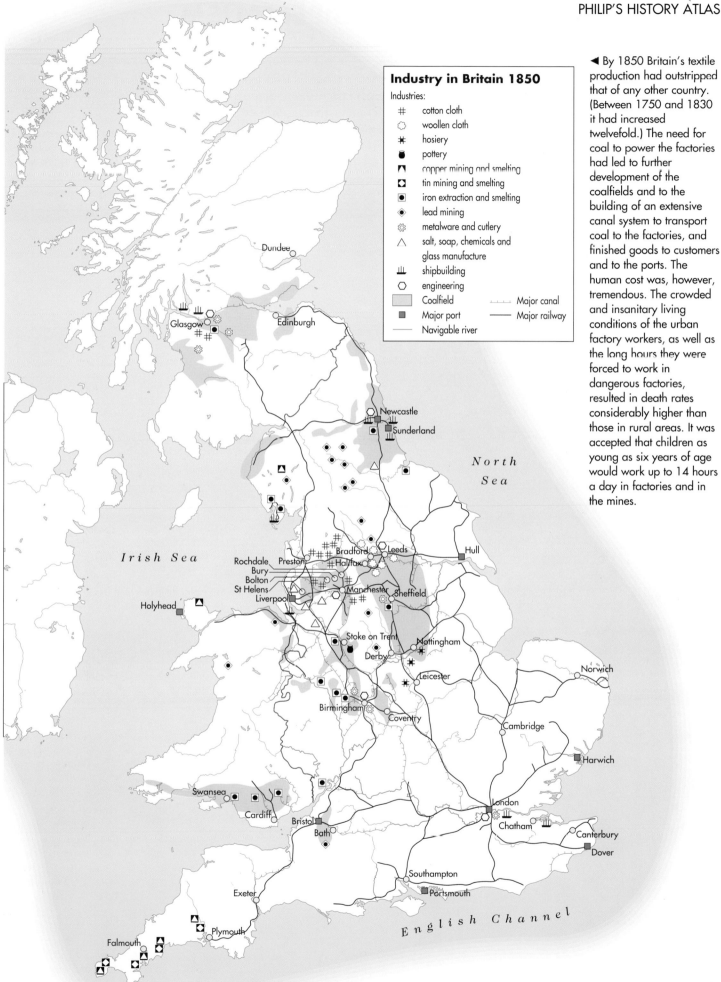

Industry in Britain 1850

Industries:

- ✳ cotton cloth
- ⬡ woollen cloth
- ✲ hosiery
- ▆ pottery
- ⋈ copper mining and smelting
- ⬓ tin mining and smelting
- ▣ iron extraction and smelting
- ◈ lead mining
- ⚙ metalware and cutlery
- △ salt, soap, chemicals and glass manufacture
- ⌁ shipbuilding
- ⬡ engineering
- ▨ Coalfield
- ▪ Major port
- ⊶ Major canal
- — Major railway
- — Navigable river

◄ By 1850 Britain's textile production had outstripped that of any other country. (Between 1750 and 1830 it had increased twelvefold.) The need for coal to power the factories had led to further development of the coalfields and to the building of an extensive canal system to transport coal to the factories, and finished goods to customers and to the ports. The human cost was, however, tremendous. The crowded and insanitary living conditions of the urban factory workers, as well as the long hours they were forced to work in dangerous factories, resulted in death rates considerably higher than those in rural areas. It was accepted that children as young as six years of age would work up to 14 hours a day in factories and in the mines.

North Sea

Irish Sea

English Channel

Dundee
Glasgow
Edinburgh
Newcastle
Sunderland
Bradford
Leeds
Hull
Rochdale
Preston
Halifax
Bury
Bolton
St Helens
Liverpool
Manchester
Sheffield
Stoke on Trent
Nottingham
Derby
Leicester
Norwich
Birmingham
Coventry
Cambridge
Harwich
Holyhead
Swansea
Cardiff
Bristol
Bath
London
Chatham
Canterbury
Dover
Southampton
Portsmouth
Exeter
Plymouth
Falmouth

INDUSTRIALISATION AND IMPERIALISM

The Industrial Revolution, which began in Britain in the late 18th century, had spread to northwest Europe and to the eastern United States by the mid-19th century. Many of the industrialising countries benefited from the experience of British engineers, who were employed in the building of factories and in the development of the railway system. By 1900

Britain, which had been unrivalled in 1850, had been overtaken by the USA as the world's leading manufacturing nation. For many countries, industrialisation went hand in hand with imperialism. They competed to secure domination over Asia, Africa and other parts of the world, seeking new sources of raw materials and markets for their manufactured products.

▼ Industrialisation in 19th-century Europe (as is clear from the development of the rail network) started in northern France, Belgium, the Netherlands and northern Germany, and spread to Spain, Italy and Austria-Hungary as the century progressed.

Industrialisation in Europe in the 19th Century

— International boundary 1871

Major railway lines constructed:
— by 1848
— 1848–1870
--- 1870–1914

Industry c. 1870:
- coal mining
- iron working
- textile production

Industry c. 1914:
- ◎ steel
- ○ engineering
- ⚓ shipbuilding
- ◇ chemicals
- ⚡ electrical industry

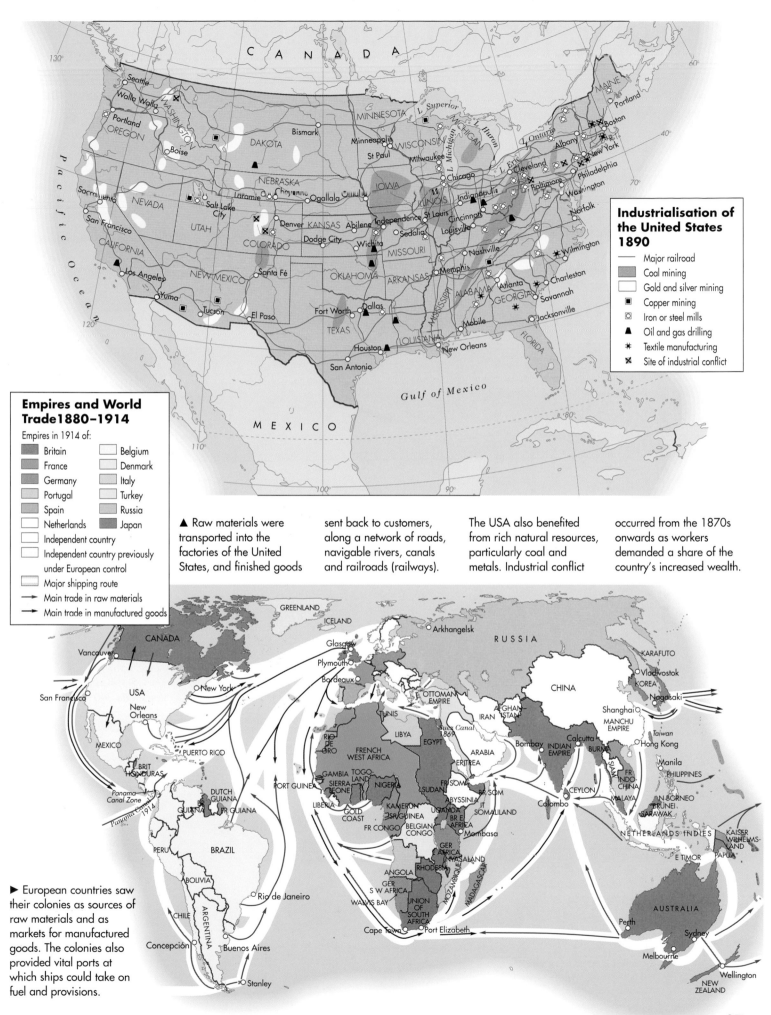

Industrialisation of the United States 1890

— Major railroad
▨ Coal mining
▢ Gold and silver mining
■ Copper mining
◉ Iron or steel mills
▲ Oil and gas drilling
✳ Textile manufacturing
✖ Site of industrial conflict

Empires and World Trade 1880–1914

Empires in 1914 of:
- Britain
- France
- Germany
- Portugal
- Spain
- Netherlands
- Independent country
- Independent country previously under European control
- Major shipping route
→ Main trade in raw materials
→ Main trade in manufactured goods
- Belgium
- Denmark
- Italy
- Turkey
- Russia
- Japan

▲ Raw materials were transported into the factories of the United States, and finished goods sent back to customers, along a network of roads, navigable rivers, canals and railroads (railways). The USA also benefited from rich natural resources, particularly coal and metals. Industrial conflict occurred from the 1870s onwards as workers demanded a share of the country's increased wealth.

► European countries saw their colonies as sources of raw materials and as markets for manufactured goods. The colonies also provided vital ports at which ships could take on fuel and provisions.

37

BUILD-UP TO THE FIRST WORLD WAR

The outbreak of war in 1914 was the result of a number of factors. The creation by 1871 of a militarily powerful and rapidly industrialising Germany was seen as threatening by France, Russia and the United Kingdom. Germany's alliances with Austria-Hungary in the early 1880s supported this view and prompted France, which had lost Alsace-Lorraine following defeat by Germany in the war of 1870–71, to ally itself with Russia in 1893. The UK, which had pursued an isolationist policy since the early years of the 19th century, briefly considered allying with Germany, but became alarmed by that country's huge military investment, and decided to side with France and Russia. This system of alliances might have resulted in a peaceful balance of power but for competition between Austria and Russia for control of the Balkans that led ultimately to the outbreak of war across Europe and the Middle East.

European Alliances 1882
- Country in Three Emperors' Alliance 1881
- Country in Triple Alliance 1882

The Balkans 1878–1914
- – – – Border of country or province 1878
- ——— Border of country 1914
- Austro-Hungarian Empire 1878
- Administered by Austria-Hungary from 1878
- Ottoman Empire 1878
- *1817* Date of autonomy within Ottoman Empire
- **1878** Date of independence from Ottoman Empire

▲ The lack of trust between the nations of central Europe was demonstrated when Germany first made an alliance with Russia, and then a pact with Italy guaranteeing that country's neutrality if Russia were to attack Germany. The Triple Alliance held until war broke out, when Italy remained neutral and eventually sided with France and the UK.

◄ The Balkans were under Ottoman rule for more than 300 years, but when the power of the Ottomans declined in the 19th century, Austria-Hungary and Russia both saw a chance to extend their empires. Bosnia was annexed by Austria in 1908. When, however, a Bosnian Serb assassinated the Austrian Archduke Ferdinand and the Austrians attempted to crush the Serb nationalists, Russia intervened.

► When war broke out in the Balkans, the system of European alliances ensured that all the major powers became embroiled.

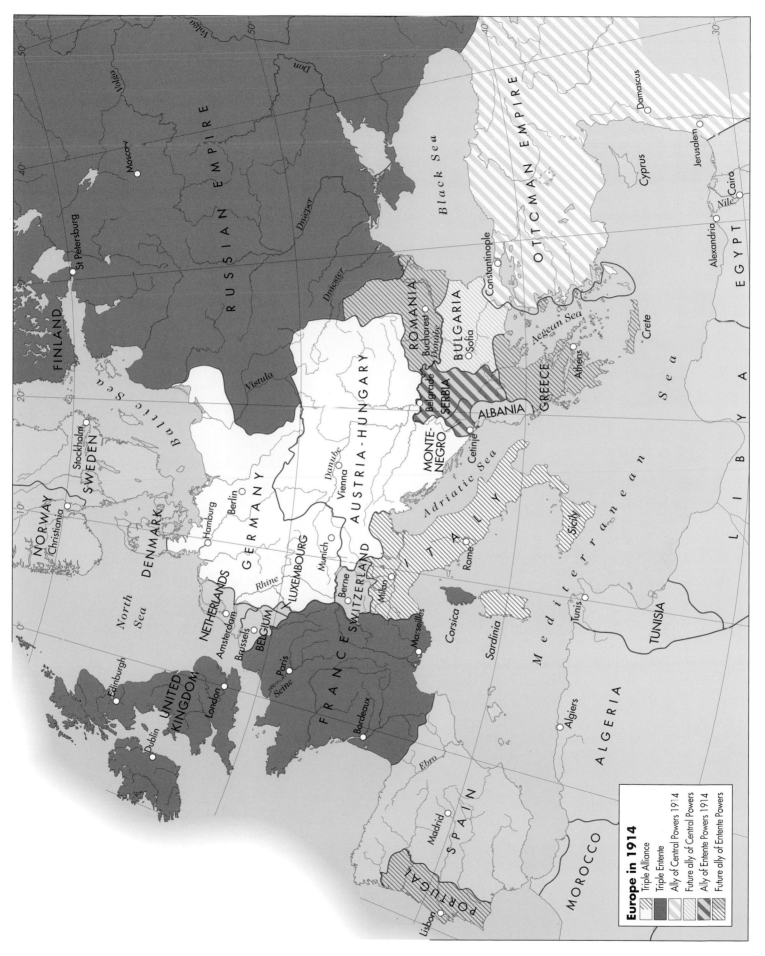

Europe in 1914

Triple Alliance
Triple Entente
Ally of Central Powers 1914
Future ally of Central Powers
Ally of Entente Powers 1914
Future ally of Entente Powers

THE FIRST WORLD WAR 1914–18

The First World War broke out on 28 July 1914 when Austria-Hungary declared war on Serbia, following the assassination of Archduke Ferdinand by a Serbian nationalist. Russia backed Serbia and began mobilising its troops, and Germany swiftly declared war on Russia and France in support of Austria-Hungary. The United Kingdom declared war on 4 August as Germany stated its aim of launching an attack on France through neutral Belgium. Over the following three years more nations from around the world became embroiled, although the main

fighting took place in Europe and the Middle East. Altogether, 32 nations declared war, the majority of them siding with the original Entente Powers (France, UK and Russia). Italy at first remained neutral, despite being allied to Germany, but in 1915, tempted by the promise of Austrian territory, joined the war on the side of the Entente Powers. The USA declared war on Germany in April 1917, following attacks by German submarines on its merchant ships. US troops and ammunition proved decisive in defeating the Germans on the Western Front.

▼ The war in Europe was waged on many fronts. The Germans advanced into Russia and in 1917 the new communist regime there surrendered. In Arabia a British Empire force from India confronted troops of the Ottoman Empire. Fighting took place in Italy between Austria-Hungary and Italy, and also in the Balkans and eastern Europe.

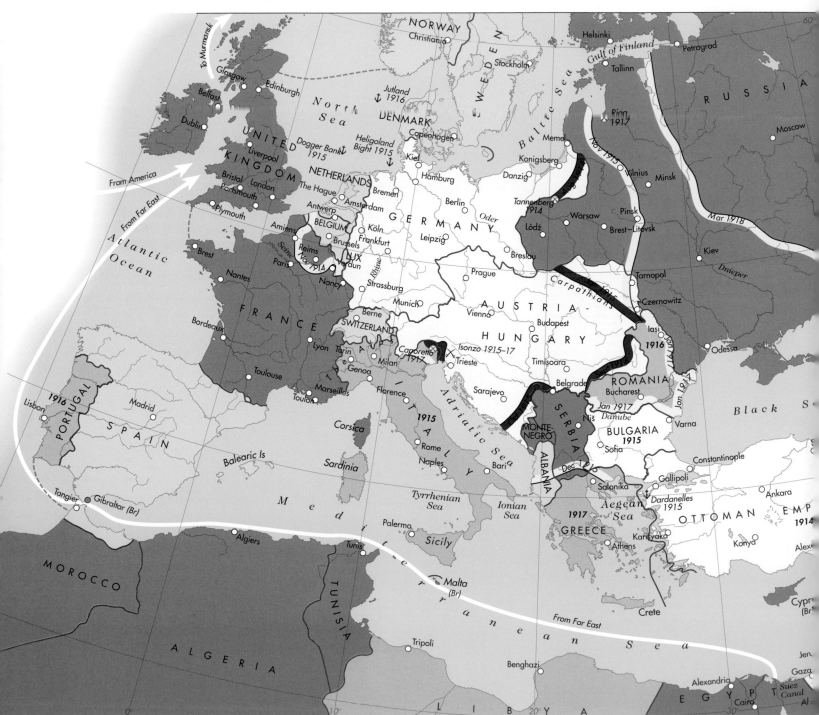

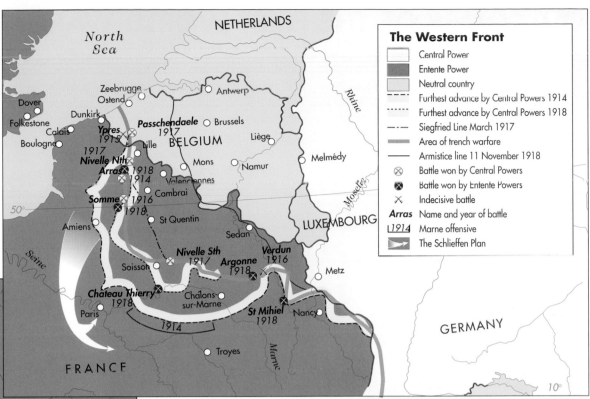

▶ On the Western Front a German advance in 1914 was repulsed, and from 1915 until 1918 the position of the two sides remained virtually static, despite the loss of millions of lives. A German advance early in 1918 was initially successful, but the Entente Powers drove the Germans back, and they agreed to an armistice on 11 November 1918.

The Western Front

☐	Central Power
■	Entente Power
☐	Neutral country
– – –	Furthest advance by Central Powers 1914
· · · · ·	Furthest advance by Central Powers 1918
– · – ·	Siegfried Line March 1917
▬▬	Area of trench warfare
——	Armistice line 11 November 1918
⊗	Battle won by Central Powers
⊗	Battle won by Entente Powers
✕	Indecisive battle
Arras	Name and year of battle
⌐1914	Marne offensive
➤	The Schlieffen Plan

The War in Europe and the Middle East

——	Borders in 1914	■	Furthest advance by Entente Powers on date marked
☐	Central Powers		
⊡1915	Neutral state that joined Central Powers, with date	⊗	Battle won by Central Powers
■	Entente Powers (including colonies)	⊗	Battle won by Entente Powers
⊡1914	Neutral state that joined Entente Powers, with date	✕	Indecisive battle
☐	Country that remained neutral	↨	Naval engagement
——	Furthest advance by Central Powers on date marked	➤	Allied convoy routes
		– – –	Naval blockade of Central Powers

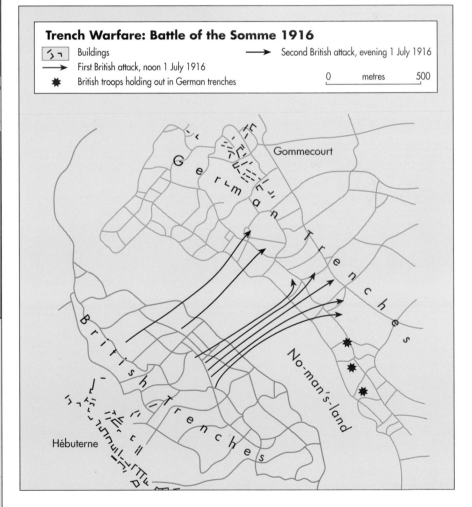

Trench Warfare: Battle of the Somme 1916

⌐⌐	Buildings	→	Second British attack, evening 1 July 1916
→	First British attack, noon 1 July 1916		
✱	British troops holding out in German trenches		

0   metres   500

▲ At the end of 1914 the two sides dug a network of trenches, sometimes only 200 metres apart, in which the soldiers ate and slept.

Shells were fired across 'no-man's-land' into the trenches; soldiers climbing out of a trench were likely to be machine-gunned.

The British launched an attack in the Somme area on 1 July 1916, and on the first day alone over 20,000 British soldiers died.

OUTCOMES OF THE FIRST WORLD WAR

Two months after the armistice of November 1918, the leaders of the victorious Entente Powers (France, the United Kingdom, Italy, the United States and Japan) met at the Paris Peace Conference. Here they decided on the principles that should govern the peace treaties to be made with the defeated Central Powers (Germany,

Austria-Hungary, the Ottoman Empire, Bulgaria and Hungary). Russia, an original member of the Entente when still under tsarist rule, had already made peace with Germany in the Treaty of Brest-Litovsk of March 1918. This had followed the Bolshevik Revolution of October 1917, during which the tsar had been overthrown.

▼ From 1918 to 1920 Bolshevik (communist) Russia was attacked by the tsarist White Russian army and foreign troops. Poland used the opportunity to gain territory from Russia on its eastern border.

The Russian Revolution and Civil War 1917–20

- – – Boundary of the Russian Empire 1914
- —— German occupation line March 1918
- → White Russian and interventionist attacks

Interventionists:
- **C** Canadian
- **G** Greek
- **US** American
- **F** French
- **B** British

- Area controlled by Bolsheviks October 1919
- Polish advance into Russia May 1920
- Russian advance into Poland August 1920
- – – USSR-Polish boundary established October 1920 by Treaty of Riga
- —— Other international boundaries 1922
- Areas lost to Russia 1914–21

Treaty Settlements in Europe 1919–23

——	Boundary 1926
- - -	Pre-war boundary
■	Territory administered by League of Nations
▨	Demilitarised zone
1918	Date of independence
——	Internationalised river

Europe in 1914

☐	Russian Empire
▨	Austro-Hungarian Empire

▲ The peace treaties made following the war radically altered the map of Europe. Under the Treaty of Versailles, Germany was considerably reduced in size, losing territory to Poland in the east and to France in the west. A 'buffer zone' was created along the Rhine, from which German troops were prohibited. The Treaty of Saint-Germain broke up the empire of Austria-Hungary into smaller national states. The Treaty of Versailles also called for the creation of the League of Nations. It was hoped that the League, which was based in Geneva, with member states from around the world, would enable disputes to be solved peacefully, by negotiation.

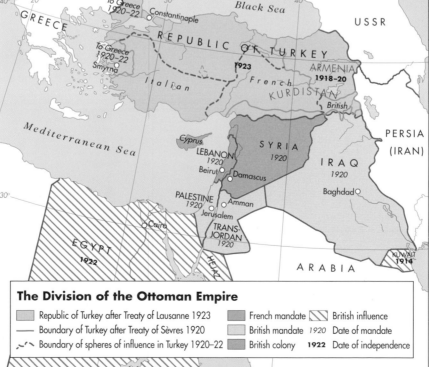

The Division of the Ottoman Empire

▨ Republic of Turkey after Treaty of Lausanne 1923	▨ French mandate	▨ British influence
—— Boundary of Turkey after Treaty of Sèvres 1920	☐ British mandate *1920* Date of mandate	
·—·— Boundary of spheres of influence in Turkey 1920–22	▨ British colony **1922** Date of independence	

◄ Under the Treaty of Sèvres of 1920, the Ottoman Empire was abolished and Anatolia divided into 'spheres of influence'. However, Mustafa Kemal (later known as 'Atatürk', father of Turkey) led a successful uprising that drove out foreign troops. The Treaty of Lausanne of 1923 recognised the modern state of Turkey. In the Middle East, ex-Ottoman territory was divided by the League of Nations into 'mandates'. These allowed European countries to administer a territory, prior to granting it independence.

THE GREAT DEPRESSION

The Great Depression of 1929–33 was the most severe economic crisis of modern times. Millions of people lost their jobs, and many farmers and businesses were bankrupted. Every country – industrial nations and those supplying the raw materials for factories – was affected. The economies of Germany and the United States

were the worst hit. The total value of goods produced by their factories was halved, and between a quarter and a third of their industrial labour force was registered as unemployed by 1932. In the United Kingdom businesses and industries also collapsed, and the already high unemployment rate was doubled.

▼ Northeast Europe was especially badly affected by the Depression. The rate of recovery varied, with unemployment reaching its peak in most countries in 1932, but continuing to rise in others until 1934.

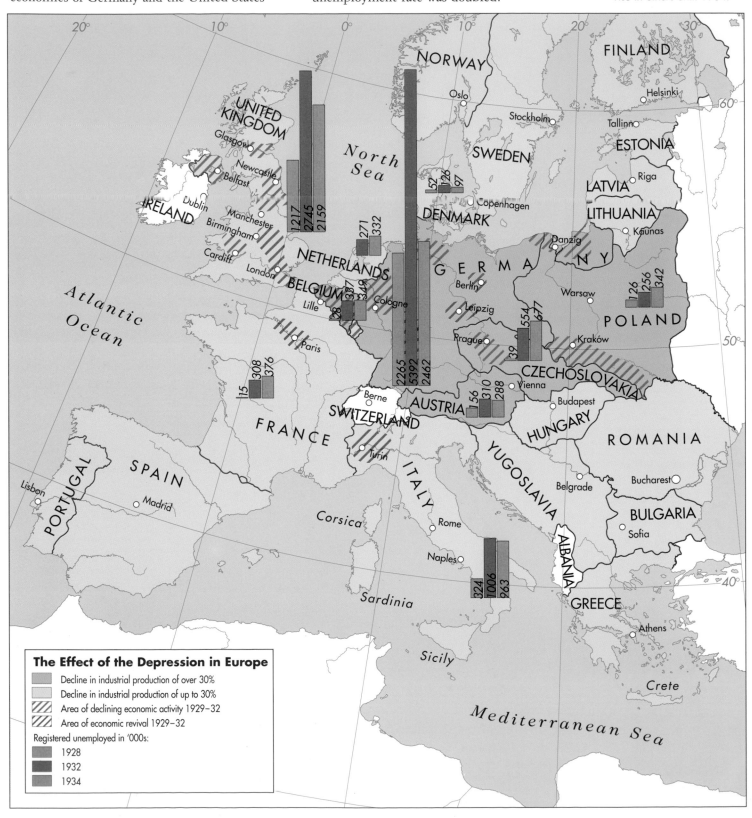

The Effect of the Depression in Europe

- Decline in industrial production of over 30%
- Decline in industrial production of up to 30%
- Area of declining economic activity 1929–32
- Area of economic revival 1929–32

Registered unemployed in '000s:
- 1928
- 1932
- 1934

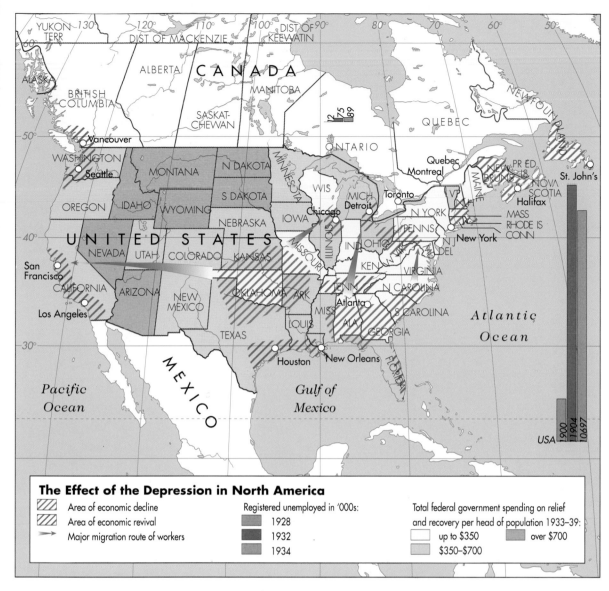

During the 1920s the United States and Canada became increasingly prosperous, but in the Wall Street Crash of October 1929 the value of shares plummeted and millions of investors lost their money. Lack of funds for investment in industry resulted in the value of goods produced declining by 50% in the USA and Canada between 1928 and 1932, thus reducing the amount of money available for reinvestment. In 1930 the Democrat Franklin D. Roosevelt was elected US President. Under his 'New Deal', government money was spent on projects intended to provide employment.

▼ The industries of the USA, Europe and Japan were supplied with raw materials from around the world, so an industrial decline had a global impact. Worst hit were Latin American countries, with China and Malaya also badly affected.

The Effect of the Depression in North America

- ▨ Area of economic decline
- ▨ Area of economic revival
- → Major migration route of workers

Registered unemployed in '000s:
- 1928
- 1932
- 1934

Total federal government spending on relief and recovery per head of population 1933–39:
- up to $350
- $350–$700
- over $700

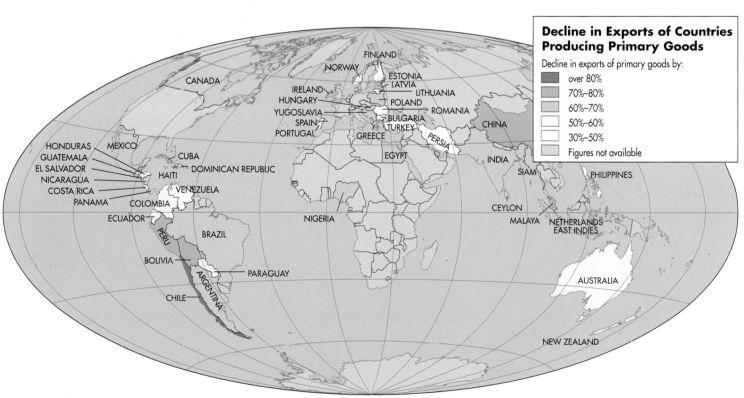

Decline in Exports of Countries Producing Primary Goods

Decline in exports of primary goods by:
- over 80%
- 70%–80%
- 60%–70%
- 50%–60%
- 30%–50%
- Figures not available

THE RISE OF FASCISM

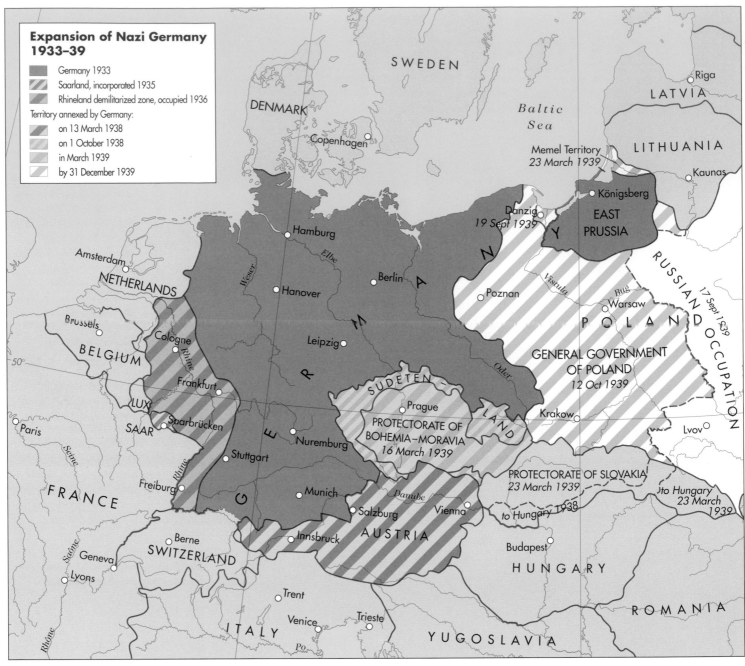

Expansion of Nazi Germany 1933–39

- Germany 1933
- Saarland, incorporated 1935
- Rhineland demilitarized zone, occupied 1936

Territory annexed by Germany:
- on 13 March 1938
- on 1 October 1938
- in March 1939
- by 31 December 1939

SWEDEN

DENMARK

Copenhagen

Baltic Sea

Riga

LATVIA

LITHUANIA

Memel Territory 23 March 1939

Kaunas

Königsberg

EAST PRUSSIA

Danzig 19 Sept 1939

Hamburg

Elbe

Weser

NETHERLANDS

Amsterdam

Berlin

Hanover

Poznan

Vistula

Warsaw

Bug

POLAND

RUSSIAN OCCUPATION

17 Sept 1939

Brussels

BELGIUM

Cologne

Rhine

Leipzig

G E R M A N Y

GENERAL GOVERNMENT OF POLAND 12 Oct 1939

Frankfurt

LUX

SAAR

Saarbrücken

Paris

Seine

SUDETEN-LAND

Prague

PROTECTORATE OF BOHEMIA–MORAVIA 16 March 1939

Oder

Krakow

Lvov

Nuremburg

Stuttgart

Freiburg

Rhine

FRANCE

PROTECTORATE OF SLOVAKIA 23 March 1939

to Hungary 1938

to Hungary 23 March 1939

Munich

Danube

Salzburg

Vienna

AUSTRIA

Budapest

HUNGARY

Berne

SWITZERLAND

Innsbruck

Geneva

Saône

Lyons

Trent

ROMANIA

Rhône

ITALY

Venice

Trieste

YUGOSLAVIA

Po

ascism was a political movement that became popular in Europe during the 1920s and 1930s, a time of extreme hardship for working people. The fascist parties in Italy and Germany attracted supporters by promising to rebuild the economies of their countries, and to provide work for all. During the 1930s the German and Italian governments invested heavily in the manufacture of armaments. They also created jobs in large-scale engineering projects such as the building of roads and power stations.

Mussolini was elected to power in Italy in 1922, but over the next few years he took steps to abolish all political parties apart from the fascists. Adopting the title of 'Il Duce' or 'the

leader', he became a dictator. The Nazi Party in Germany, led by Hitler, followed a similar course after Hitler became Chancellor in 1933.

Fascist leaders aimed to unite people from all sections of society – agricultural and industrial workers, the middle-classes and the land- and factory-owners – and to encourage them to think of their nation as better than any other. This unity came at a price, however. The Nazi Party, under Hitler, saw the Germans as a super-race, and excluded from society people whom they considered physically or mentally 'defective'. Jewish people were blamed for Germany's economic problems: their businesses were ruined and they were attacked and imprisoned.

▲ One of Hitler's priorities was to regain territory lost to Germany after the First World War and to unite all German-speaking people. In 1938 Germany annexed Austria and, following the signing of the Munich Agreement with the UK and France, the Sudetenland. German troops took control of the rest of Czechoslovakia in March 1939 and their attack on Poland in September 1939 caused the outbreak of the Second World War.

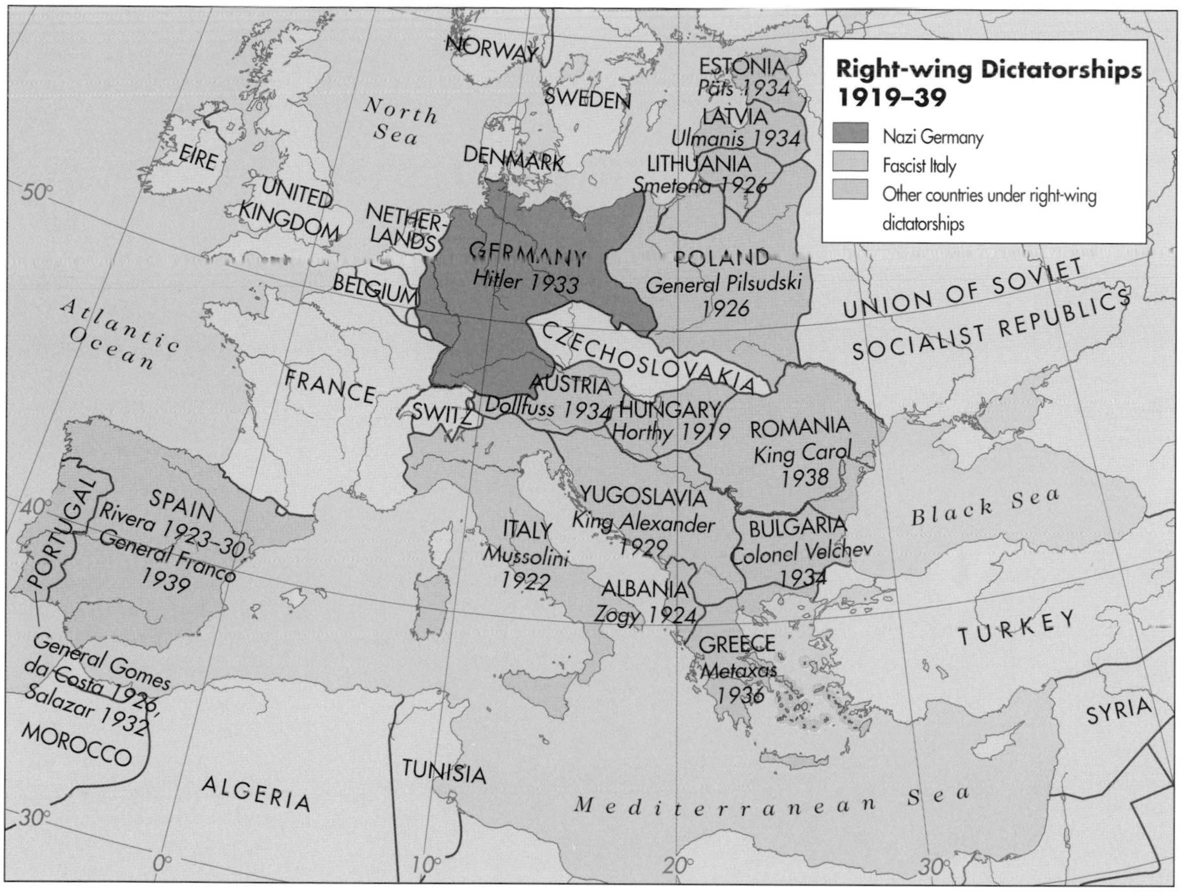
Right-wing Dictatorships 1919–39
Nazi Germany
Fascist Italy
Other countries under right-wing dictatorships
NORWAY
SWEDEN
ESTONIA Päts 1934
LATVIA Ulmanis 1934
LITHUANIA Smetona 1926
North Sea
DENMARK
EIRE
UNITED KINGDOM
NETHERLANDS
GERMANY Hitler 1933
POLAND General Pilsudski 1926
BELGIUM
UNION OF SOVIET SOCIALIST REPUBLICS
Atlantic Ocean
CZECHOSLOVAKIA
FRANCE
AUSTRIA Dollfuss 1934
SWITZ
HUNGARY Horthy 1919
ROMANIA King Carol 1938
SPAIN Rivera 1923–30, General Franco 1939
PORTUGAL
YUGOSLAVIA King Alexander 1929
ITALY Mussolini 1922
BULGARIA Colonel Velchev 1934
Black Sea
ALBANIA Zogy 1924
GREECE Metaxas 1936
TURKEY
General Gomes da Costa 1926, Salazar 1932
MOROCCO
SYRIA
ALGERIA
TUNISIA
Mediterranean Sea
50°
40°
30°
0°
10°
20°
30°

◀ Fascism developed in its most extreme form in Germany and Italy, but right-wing dictators (who adopted some of the principles of Fascism) came to power across Europe. Czechoslovakia stood out as a beacon of democracy in central Europe.

▼ The Spanish Civil War started in 1936 when an army led by General Franco (the Nationalists) invaded Spain from Morocco, to oust the democratically elected Popular Front government led by Azaña (the Republicans). With military help from fascist Italy and Germany, both of which used the war to test their latest weapons, Franco's army defeated the Republicans in April 1939. Franco then established a dictatorship that was to last until 1975.

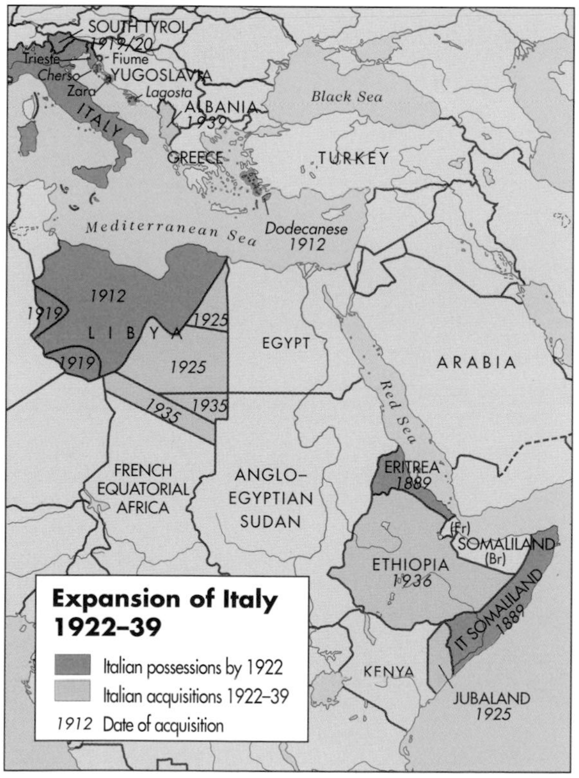
Expansion of Italy 1922–39
Italian possessions by 1922
Italian acquisitions 1922–39
1912 Date of acquisition
SOUTH TYROL 1919/20
Trieste
Fiume
Cherso
YUGOSLAVIA
Zara
Lagosta
ALBANIA 1939
ITALY
Black Sea
GREECE
TURKEY
Mediterranean Sea
Dodecanese 1912
1912
1919
LIBYA
1925
1919
1925
1935
1935
EGYPT
ARABIA
Red Sea
FRENCH EQUATORIAL AFRICA
ANGLO-EGYPTIAN SUDAN
ERITREA 1889
(Fr)
SOMALILAND (Br)
ETHIOPIA 1936
IT SOMALILAND 1889
KENYA
JUBALAND 1925

▲ Mussolini sought to revive Italian national pride and to increase his own personal power by extending Italy's territory on the Adriatic and enlarging its African empire. His invasion of Ethiopia provoked outrage from countries worldwide.

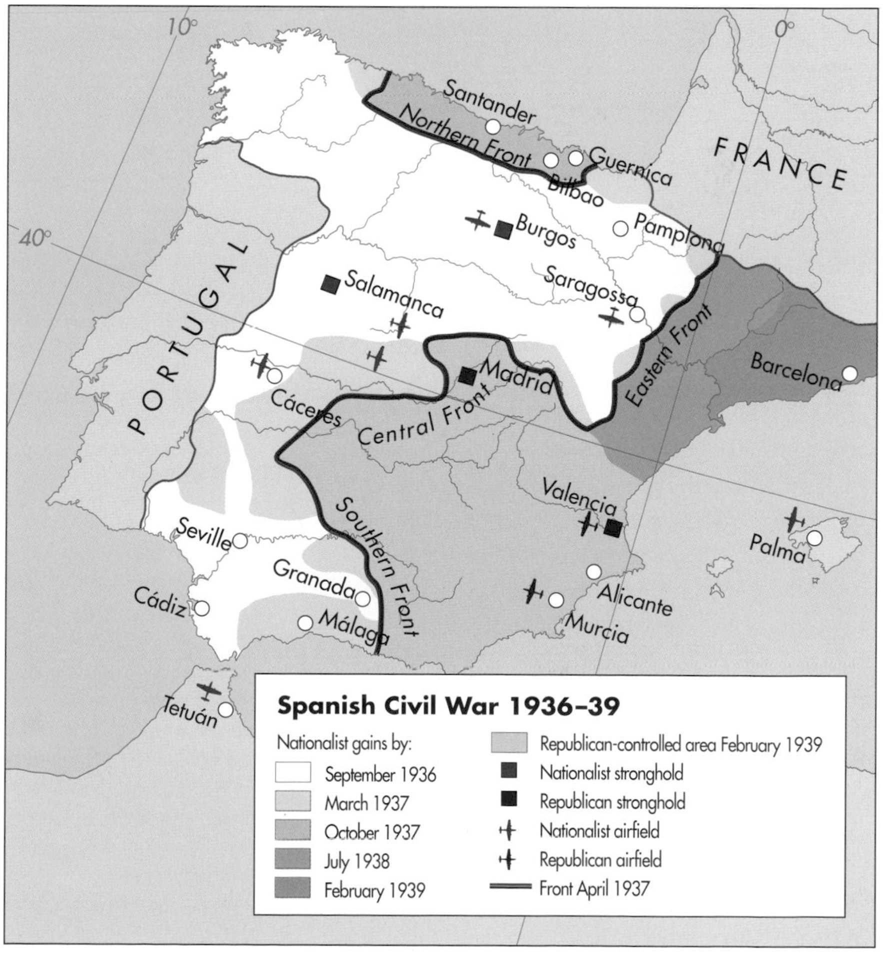
Spanish Civil War 1936–39
Nationalist gains by:
September 1936
March 1937
October 1937
July 1938
February 1939
Republican-controlled area February 1939
Nationalist stronghold
Republican stronghold
Nationalist airfield
Republican airfield
Front April 1937
10°
0°
40°
Santander
Northern Front
Guernica
Bilbao
FRANCE
Burgos
Pamplona
PORTUGAL
Salamanca
Saragossa
Eastern Front
Madrid
Barcelona
Cáceres
Central Front
Valencia
Southern Front
Seville
Palma
Granada
Alicante
Cádiz
Málaga
Murcia
Tetuán

THE SECOND WORLD WAR IN EUROPE 1939–45

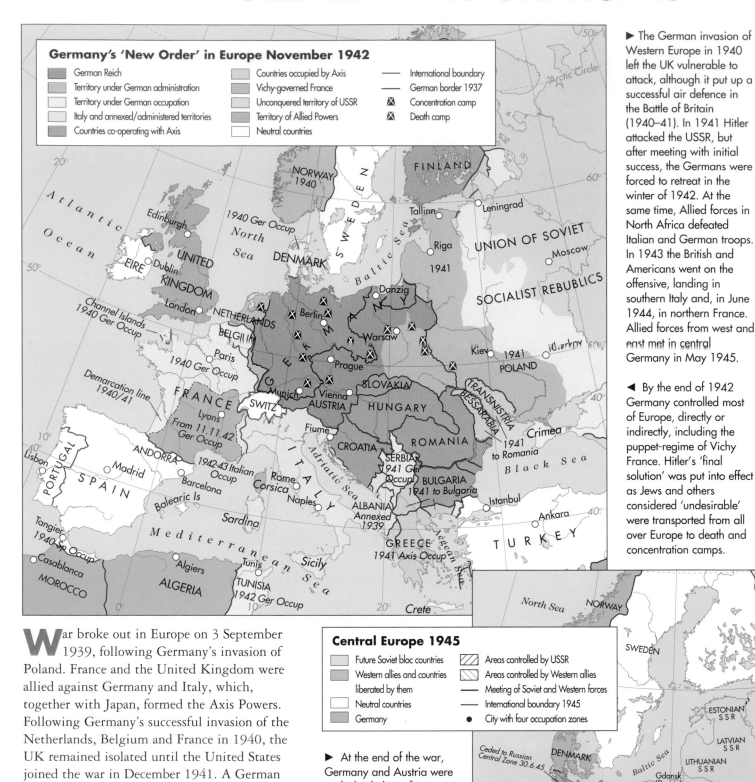

Germany's 'New Order' in Europe November 1942

- German Reich
- Territory under German administration
- Territory under German occupation
- Italy and annexed/administered territories
- Countries co-operating with Axis
- Countries occupied by Axis
- Vichy-governed France
- Unconquered territory of USSR
- Territory of Allied Powers
- Neutral countries
- —— International boundary
- —— German border 1937
- ☒ Concentration camp
- ☒ Death camp

▶ The German invasion of Western Europe in 1940 left the UK vulnerable to attack, although it put up a successful air defence in the Battle of Britain (1940–41). In 1941 Hitler attacked the USSR, but after meeting with initial success, the Germans were forced to retreat in the winter of 1942. At the same time, Allied forces in North Africa defeated Italian and German troops. In 1943 the British and Americans went on the offensive, landing in southern Italy and, in June 1944, in northern France. Allied forces from west and east met in central Germany in May 1945.

◀ By the end of 1942 Germany controlled most of Europe, directly or indirectly, including the puppet-regime of Vichy France. Hitler's 'final solution' was put into effect as Jews and others considered 'undesirable' were transported from all over Europe to death and concentration camps.

Central Europe 1945

- Future Soviet bloc countries
- Western allies and countries liberated by them
- Neutral countries
- Germany
- ▨ Areas controlled by USSR
- ▨ Areas controlled by Western allies
- —— Meeting of Soviet and Western forces
- —— International boundary 1945
- ● City with four occupation zones

War broke out in Europe on 3 September 1939, following Germany's invasion of Poland. France and the United Kingdom were allied against Germany and Italy, which, together with Japan, formed the Axis Powers. Following Germany's successful invasion of the Netherlands, Belgium and France in 1940, the UK remained isolated until the United States joined the war in December 1941. A German invasion of the Soviet Union in 1941 was at first successful, but foundered in the winter of 1942–43. Following the landing of Allied forces on Italian soil, the Italians surrendered in September 1943 and declared war on Germany. German troops continued to put up a strong defence in Italy, on the Eastern Front and against the Allied force that landed in France in 1944, but the Allies eventually forced a German surrender on 7 May 1945.

▶ At the end of the war, Germany and Austria were each divided into four 'zones of occupation', controlled by the Western allies (the UK, the USA and France) and the USSR. The cities of Berlin and Vienna were also divided into four zones. The USSR withdrew from Austria in 1955, but retained indirect control over its German sector until 1989.

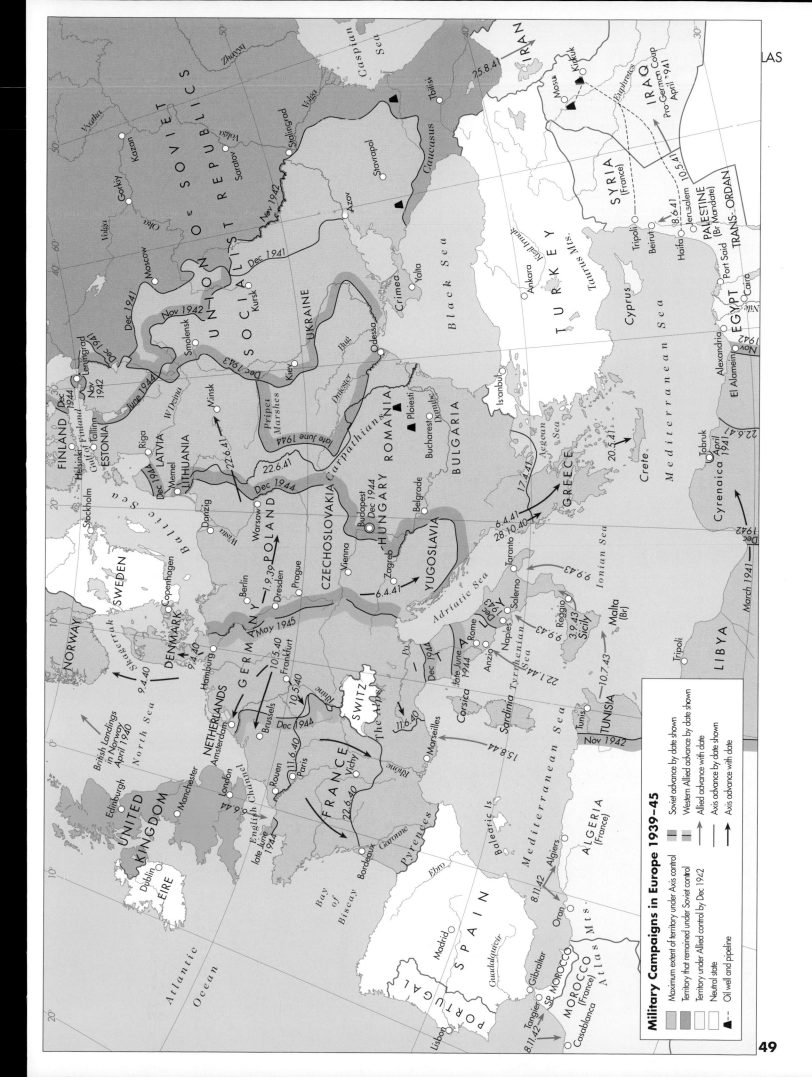

Military Campaigns in Europe 1939-45

Maximum extent of territory under Axis control

Territory that remained under Soviet control

Territory under Allied control by Dec 1942

Neutral state

▲- - Oil well and pipeline

Soviet advance by date shown

Western Allied advance by date shown

Allied advance with date

Axis advance by date shown

Axis advance with date

THE SECOND WORLD WAR IN ASIA

The war in Asia arose following Japanese incursions into China during the 1930s. Allied with Germany and Italy since September 1940, and threatened with an oil embargo, the Japanese launched a pre-emptive strike against the US fleet in Pearl Harbour, Hawaii, in December 1941. At the same time, they attacked the British in Hong Kong and Dutch territories in Malaysia. For the next six months the Japanese swept through Southeast Asia, but following a surprise defeat by the US navy at the Battle of Midway in June 1942 the tide began to

turn. Slowly the US forces, assisted by those from Australia and New Zealand, pushed the Japanese back, while UK and Indian troops defended India. Fighting continued into 1945, with the USA launching bombing raids on Japan. When the Japanese did not surrender, however, the USA decided to use the newly developed atomic bomb. The first bomb was dropped on Hiroshima on 6 August, killing or injuring 130,000 civilians. The dropping of a second bomb on Nagasaki led to the Japanese surrender on 15 August 1945.

▼ The rate of the Japanese advance took the Allied forces by surprise. UK, Dutch and US territories fell like dominoes. French Indochina, under the Vichy government, was sympathetic to Japan, as was Thailand. Japan ruled over its new territories with an iron fist and engaged in atrocities against the native populations and European prisoners of war.

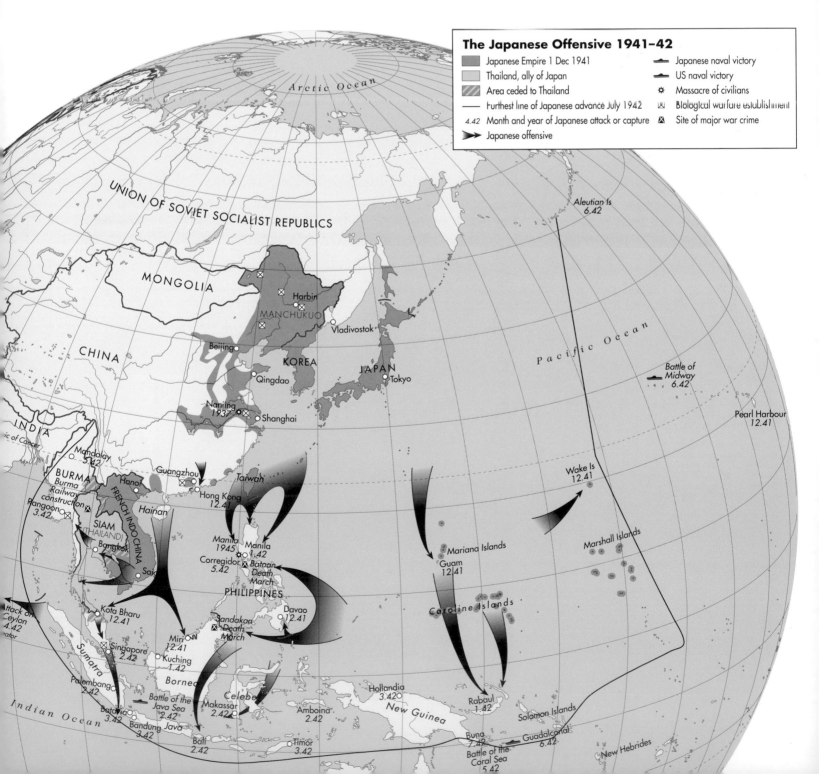

The Japanese Offensive 1941–42

- ▨ Japanese Empire 1 Dec 1941
- ▨ Thailand, ally of Japan
- ▨ Area ceded to Thailand
- — Furthest line of Japanese advance July 1942
- 4.42 Month and year of Japanese attack or capture
- ➤ Japanese offensive
- ⚓ Japanese naval victory
- ⚓ US naval victory
- � Massacre of civilians
- ⊠ Biological warfare establishment
- ⊠ Site of major war crime

► During the early 1930s Japan took advantage of a lack of strong government in China to invade the northeast of the country. Outright war was declared between the two countries in 1937 and the Japanese continued to gain ground until 1945. They were driven back largely by Chinese communist troops in the south and west, and by the Soviet army in Manchukuo.

▼ It took the Allies over three years to regain territory that had fallen to Japan over a six-month period. Indeed, when Japan surrendered on 15 August 1945, its troops still occupied a large part of Southeast Asia.

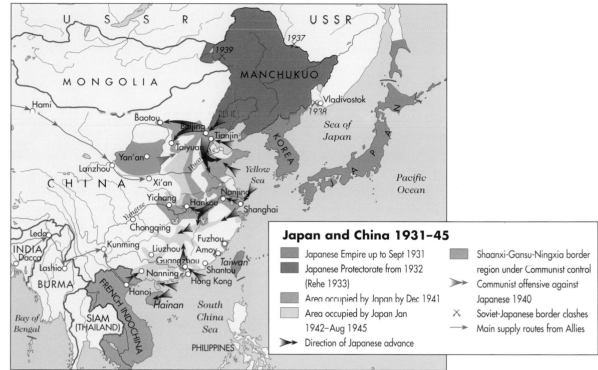

Japan and China 1931–45

▨ Japanese Empire up to Sept 1931	▨ Shaanxi-Gansu-Ningxia border region under Communist control
▨ Japanese Protectorate from 1932 (Rehe 1933)	➤ Communist offensive against Japanese 1940
▨ Area occupied by Japan by Dec 1941	✕ Soviet-Japanese border clashes
▨ Area occupied by Japan Jan 1942–Aug 1945	→ Main supply routes from Allies
➤ Direction of Japanese advance	

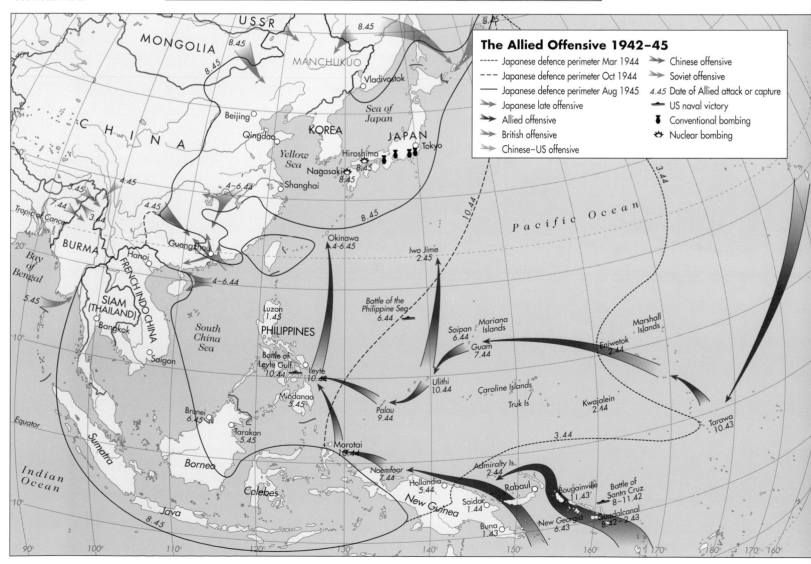

The Allied Offensive 1942–45

----- Japanese defence perimeter Mar 1944	➤ Chinese offensive
- - - Japanese defence perimeter Oct 1944	➤ Soviet offensive
—— Japanese defence perimeter Aug 1945	4.45 Date of Allied attack or capture
➤ Japanese late offensive	⚓ US naval victory
➤ Allied offensive	♟ Conventional bombing
➤ British offensive	✿ Nuclear bombing
➤ Chinese–US offensive	

THE COLD WAR

The Cold War was a political and diplomatic conflict in the years 1947–91 between the United States and its capitalist allies within NATO, and the communist Warsaw Pact countries led by the Soviet Union. It took the form of an arms and space race, the provision of economic and military aid to other countries and, occasionally, direct involvement in regional wars. The Cold War reached it height in 1962, when the Cuban missile crisis almost resulted in a third world war. It ended in 1991 with the disintegration of the East European communist governments and of the Soviet Union.

The Iron Curtain

- ▨ Countries under influence of USSR
- ▨ Non-aligned communist
- ☐ Non-communist
- — Iron Curtain
- *1947* Date when communist government was established

▲ After the Second World War an 'Iron Curtain' descended across Europe, dividing the communist regimes of Eastern Europe (which in 1955 formed the Warsaw Pact) from the rest of Europe.

► The Korean War was the bloodiest confrontation of the Cold War. After the Japanese surrender in 1945, Korea was divided along the 38th parallel. The war began with an attack by the communist north on the pro-Western south, and involved both Chinese and UN (largely US) troops. A ceasefire line held from 1953, with a permanent peace agreement still not reached in 1998.

◄ The Vietnam War began when communist North Vietnamese troops (Vietcong) attempted to overthrow the US-backed southern regime. US troops became heavily involved in 1964–73 to no avail, and in 1975 North and South were reunited under communist control.

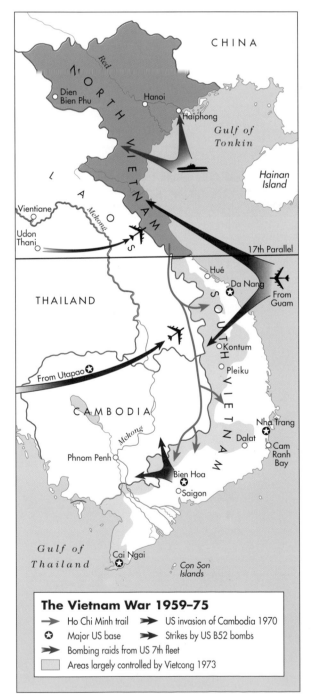

The Vietnam War 1959–75

- → Ho Chi Minh trail
- ✪ Major US base
- ⇥ Bombing raids from US 7th fleet
- → US invasion of Cambodia 1970
- → Strikes by US B52 bombs
- ▨ Areas largely controlled by Vietcong 1973

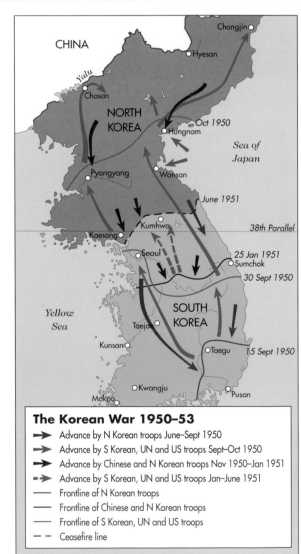

The Korean War 1950–53

- → Advance by N Korean troops June–Sept 1950
- → Advance by S Korean, UN and US troops Sept–Oct 1950
- → Advance by Chinese and N Korean troops Nov 1950–Jan 1951
- ⇢ Advance by S Korean, UN and US troops Jan–June 1951
- — Frontline of N Korean troops
- — Frontline of Chinese and N Korean troops
- — Frontline of S Korean, UN and US troops
- – – Ceasefire line

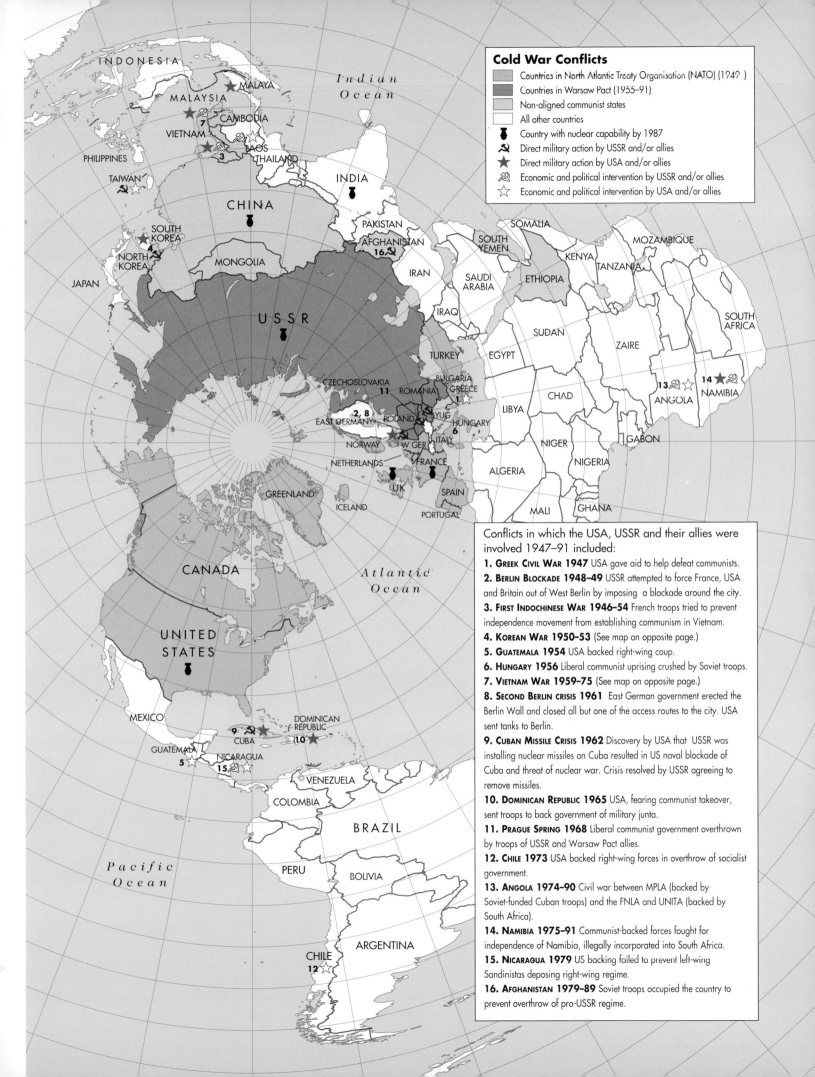

Cold War Conflicts

- Countries in North Atlantic Treaty Organisation (NATO) (1949)
- Countries in Warsaw Pact (1955–91)
- Non-aligned communist states
- All other countries
- Country with nuclear capability by 1987
- Direct military action by USSR and/or allies
- Direct military action by USA and/or allies
- Economic and political intervention by USSR and/or allies
- Economic and political intervention by USA and/or allies

Conflicts in which the USA, USSR and their allies were involved 1947–91 included:

1. GREEK CIVIL WAR 1947 USA gave aid to help defeat communists.

2. BERLIN BLOCKADE 1948–49 USSR attempted to force France, USA and Britain out of West Berlin by imposing a blockade around the city.

3. FIRST INDOCHINESE WAR 1946–54 French troops tried to prevent independence movement from establishing communism in Vietnam.

4. KOREAN WAR 1950–53 (See map on opposite page.)

5. GUATEMALA 1954 USA backed right-wing coup.

6. HUNGARY 1956 Liberal communist uprising crushed by Soviet troops.

7. VIETNAM WAR 1959–75 (See map on opposite page.)

8. SECOND BERLIN CRISIS 1961 East German government erected the Berlin Wall and closed all but one of the access routes to the city. USA sent tanks to Berlin.

9. CUBAN MISSILE CRISIS 1962 Discovery by USA that USSR was installing nuclear missiles on Cuba resulted in US naval blockade of Cuba and threat of nuclear war. Crisis resolved by USSR agreeing to remove missiles.

10. DOMINICAN REPUBLIC 1965 USA, fearing communist takeover, sent troops to back government of military junta.

11. PRAGUE SPRING 1968 Liberal communist government overthrown by troops of USSR and Warsaw Pact allies.

12. CHILE 1973 USA backed right-wing forces in overthrow of socialist government.

13. ANGOLA 1974–90 Civil war between MPLA (backed by Soviet-funded Cuban troops) and the FNLA and UNITA (backed by South Africa).

14. NAMIBIA 1975–91 Communist-backed forces fought for independence of Namibia, illegally incorporated into South Africa.

15. NICARAGUA 1979 US backing failed to prevent left-wing Sandinistas deposing right-wing regime.

16. AFGHANISTAN 1979–89 Soviet troops occupied the country to prevent overthrow of pro-USSR regime.

EUROPE AND EUROPEAN EMPIRES SINCE 1945

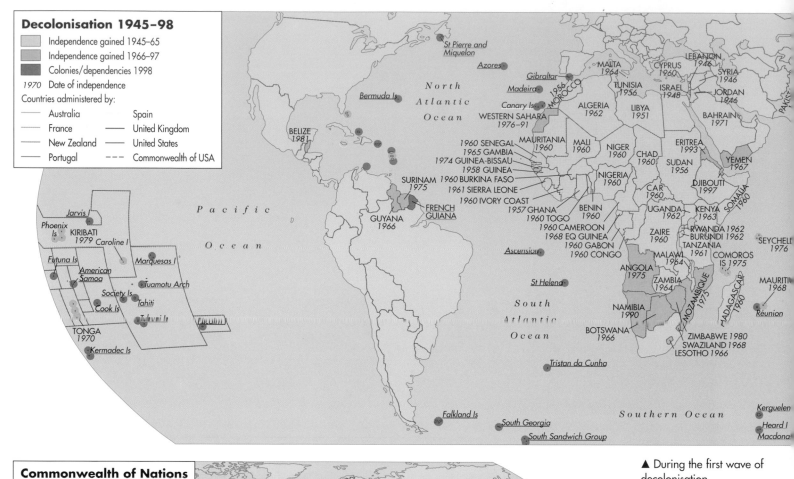

Decolonisation 1945–98

- Independence gained 1945–65
- Independence gained 1966–97
- Colonies/dependencies 1998

1970 Date of independence

Countries administered by:
- Australia
- France
- New Zealand
- Portugal
- Spain
- United Kingdom
- United States
- – – – Commonwealth of USA

St Pierre and Miquelon

North Atlantic Ocean

Azores

Bermuda Is

Gibraltar

Madeira

1956 MOROCCO

Canary Is

MALTA 1964

TUNISIA 1956

ALGERIA 1962

LIBYA 1951

CYPRUS 1960

LEBANON 1946

SYRIA 1946

ISRAEL 1948

JORDAN 1946

BAHRAIN 1971

PAKISTAN

BELIZE 1981

WESTERN SAHARA 1976–91

MAURITANIA 1960

MALI 1960

NIGER 1960

CHAD 1960

SUDAN 1956

ERITREA 1993

YEMEN 1967

1960 SENEGAL
1965 GAMBIA
1974 GUINEA-BISSAU
1958 GUINEA
1960 BURKINA FASO
1961 SIERRA LEONE
1960 IVORY COAST
1957 GHANA

SURINAM 1975

GUYANA 1966

FRENCH GUIANA

NIGERIA 1960

CAR 1960

DJIBOUTI 1997

SOMALIA 1960

1960 TOGO
1960 CAMEROON
1968 EQ GUINEA
1960 GABON
1960 CONGO

BENIN 1960

ZAIRE 1960

UGANDA 1962

RWANDA 1962
BURUNDI 1962

KENYA 1963

TANZANIA 1961

SEYCHELLES 1976

Ascension

MALAWI 1964

COMOROS IS 1975

Pacific Ocean

Jarvis I

Phoenix Is

KIRIBATI 1979

Caroline I

Futuna Is

Marquesas I

American Samoa

Tuamotu Arch

Society Is

Tahiti

Cook Is

Tuvuni In

Pitcairn

TONGA 1970

Kermadec Is

ANGOLA 1975

ZAMBIA 1964

MOZAMBIQUE 1975

MADAGASCAR 1960

MAURITIUS 1968

Réunion

St Helena

South Atlantic Ocean

NAMIBIA 1990

BOTSWANA 1966

ZIMBABWE 1980
SWAZILAND 1968
LESOTHO 1966

Tristan da Cunha

Falkland Is

South Georgia

South Sandwich Group

Southern Ocean

Kerguelen

Heard I
Macdona

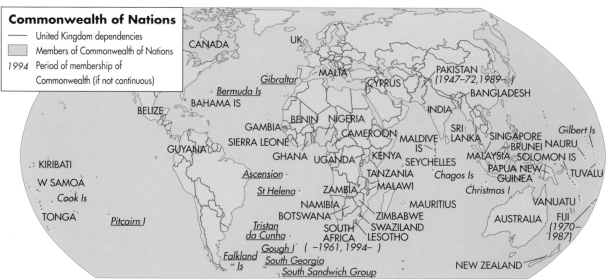

Commonwealth of Nations

- —— United Kingdom dependencies
- Members of Commonwealth of Nations
- *1994* Period of membership of Commonwealth (if not continuous)

CANADA

UK

CCANADA

Gibraltar

MALTA

CYPRUS

PAKISTAN (1947–72, 1989–)

BANGLADESH

Bermuda Is

BAHAMA IS

BELIZE

INDIA

GAMBIA

BENIN

NIGERIA

CAMEROON

SRI LANKA

MALDIVE IS

SINGAPORE

BRUNEI

NAURU

Gilbert Is

SIERRA LEONE

GUYANA

GHANA

UGANDA

KENYA

SEYCHELLES

MALAYSIA

SOLOMON IS

PAPUA NEW GUINEA

TUVALU

KIRIBATI

W SAMOA

Cook Is

TONGA

Ascension

St Helena

TANZANIA

ZAMBIA

MALAWI

Chagos Is

Christmas I

VANUATU

Pitcairn I

NAMIBIA

BOTSWANA

ZIMBABWE

SWAZILAND

LESOTHO

MAURITIUS

AUSTRALIA

FIJI (1970–1987)

Tristan da Cunha

SOUTH AFRICA

Gough I (–1961, 1994–)

Falkland Is

South Georgia

South Sandwich Group

NEW ZEALAND

▲ During the first wave of decolonisation, immediately after the Second World War (1939–45), France and Britain gave up their mandates in the Middle East. Independence in Southeast Asia resulted in the formation of the independent states of Malaysia and Indonesia. The French fought against Algerian independence, but gave up their remaining African colonies in 1960. The Portuguese resisted calls for colonial independence until 1974.

▲ The Commonwealth of Nations was founded in 1931 and is an informal organisation, the aim of which is to promote co-operation between Britain and its ex-colonies. The heads of state of the 51 member countries meet every two years to discuss issues of common concern, such as world trade and human rights.

In the period immediately after the Second World War it became clear that the European countries were not going to be able to hold on to their colonial possessions indefinitely. The native inhabitants of colonised countries demanded (and most were eventually granted) the right to govern themselves. At the same time there was a movement towards greater co-operation in Europe, in an attempt to avert another world war. The European Economic Community (EEC) was established in 1957 by the Treaty of Rome.

It aimed to abolish trade barriers between member countries, and to develop a common policy on agriculture. While the EEC (known since 1993 as the European Union) became the main trading block in Western Europe, the communist-controlled states of Eastern Europe formed their own trade organisation, known as COMECON. Since the collapse of communism in Europe and the Soviet Union, many former communist countries have, however, applied to join the European Union.

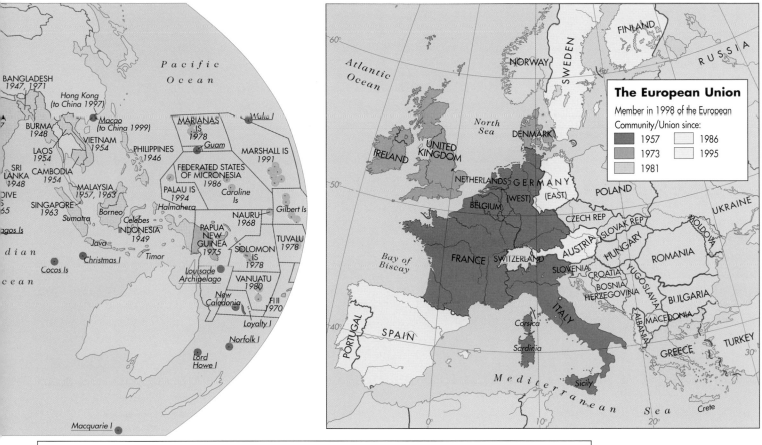

BANGLADESH *1947, 1971*
Hong Kong (to China 1997)
BURMA *1948*
Macao (to China 1999)
VIETNAM *1954*
LAOS *1954*
PHILIPPINES *1946*
SRI LANKA *1948*
CAMBODIA *1954*
MALAYSIA *1957, 1963*
SINGAPORE *1963*
Sumatra
Borneo
Celebes
INDONESIA *1949*
Java
Christmas I
Cocos Is
Timor
Halmahera

Pacific Ocean
Atlantic Ocean

MARIANAS IS *1978*
Guam
MARSHALL IS *1991*
FEDERATED STATES OF MICRONESIA *1986*
PALAU IS *1994*
Caroline Is
NAURU *1968*
Gilbert Is
SOLOMON IS *1978*
TUVALU *1978*
PAPUA NEW GUINEA *1975*
Louisade Archipelago
VANUATU *1980*
New Caledonia
FIJI *1970*
Loyalty I
Norfolk I
Lord Howe I
Wake I

Macquarie I

The European Union

Member in 1998 of the European Community/Union since:

1957	1986
1973	1995
1981	

Atlantic Ocean
North Sea
NORWAY
SWEDEN
FINLAND
RUSSIA
DENMARK
IRELAND
UNITED KINGDOM
NETHERLANDS
GERMANY (WEST)
(EAST)
POLAND
BELGIUM
CZECH REP
SLOVAK REP
UKRAINE
MOLDOVA
FRANCE
SWITZERLAND
AUSTRIA
HUNGARY
ROMANIA
Bay of Biscay
SLOVENIA
CROATIA
BOSNIA HERZEGOVINA
YUGOSLAVIA
BULGARIA
PORTUGAL
SPAIN
ITALY
Corsica
Sardinia
ALBANIA
MACEDONIA
GREECE
TURKEY
Sicily
Mediterranean Sea
Crete

Break-up of the Soviet Union since 1991

—— Border of Soviet Union until 1991
▢ Member state (with Russian Federation) of Commonwealth of Independent States (CIS)
▢ Autonomous area within independent state
▨ Russian Federation
▨ Constituent republic within Russian Federation
▨ State not member of CIS
✵ Area of armed conflict

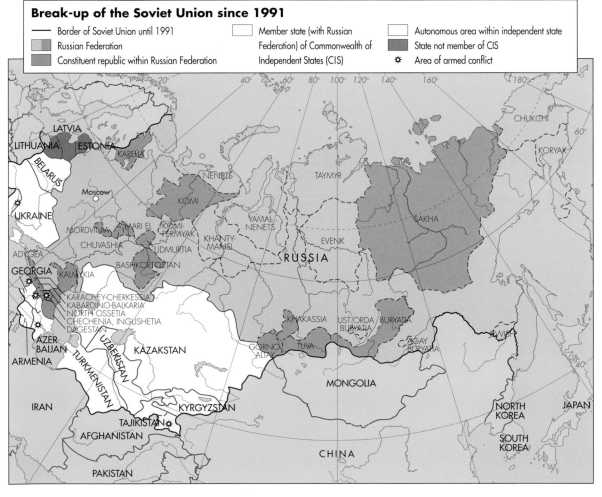

LATVIA
LITHUANIA
ESTONIA
KARELIA
BELARUS
Moscow
NENETS
UKRAINE
KOMI
TAYMYR
CHUKCHI
KORYAK
MORDVINIA
MARI EL
KOMI-PERMYAK
YAMAL NENETS
KHANTY-MANSI
SAKHA
CHUVASHIA
UDMURTIA
EVENK
ADYGEA
GEORGIA
KALMYKIA
BASHKORTOSTAN
RUSSIA
KARACHEY-CHERKESSIA
KABARDINO-BALKARIA
NORTH OSSETIA
CHECHENIA, INGUSHETIA
DAGESTAN
KHAKASSIA
UST ORDA BURYATIA
BURYATIA
AZER-BAIJAN
ARMENIA
TURKMENISTAN
UZBEKISTAN
KAZAKSTAN
GORNO-ALTAY
TUVA
AGA BURYATIA
JEWISH
IRAN
MONGOLIA
KYRGYZSTAN
TAJIKISTAN
AFGHANISTAN
CHINA
NORTH KOREA
SOUTH KOREA
JAPAN
PAKISTAN

▲ The European Economic Community originally consisted of six member countries but has expanded substantially over the years. The EEC became the European Community (EC) in 1967. Following the ratification of the Treaty of European Union at Maastricht in 1993, the organisation changed its name again to the European Union (EU).

◄ The Union of Soviet Socialist Republics (Soviet Union) broke up into independent states in 1991, following the introduction of multi-party democracy and the demise of the Communist Party. All the states, except those on the Baltic coastline, agreed to join the CIS, intended to promote common trade, economic, foreign and defence policies. In reality, however, there has been little agreement between member nations, the largest of which is Russia.

ASIA SINCE 1920

Until 1941 India and Southeast Asia were almost entirely under European rule. This situation was shattered, however, by the Japanese invasion of Southeast Asia from December 1941. When the European powers returned, following the defeat of the Japanese in 1945, they found their former colonies determined to rule themselves. The process of establishing independence took over 30 years and involved bloody conflict in Vietnam. The British government bowed to pressure for independence in India in 1947 but, because of religious conflict, divided it into Hindu India and Muslim Pakistan. Following the withdrawal of the colonial powers in Southeast Asia, most of the small states grouped together to form Malaysia (1957) and the Republic of Indonesia (1949). East Timor, made independent from Portugal in 1976, was incorporated by force into Indonesia.

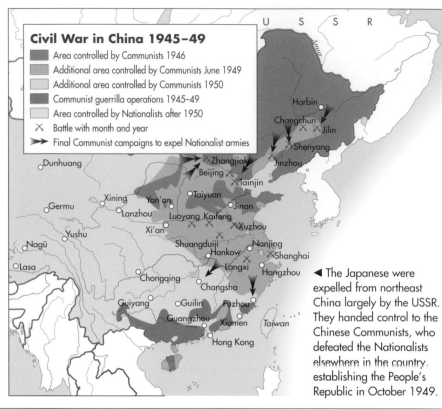

Civil War in China 1945–49

- Area controlled by Communists 1946
- Additional area controlled by Communists June 1949
- Additional area controlled by Communists 1950
- Communist guerrilla operations 1945–49
- Area controlled by Nationalists after 1950
- ✕ Battle with month and year
- ➤ Final Communist campaigns to expel Nationalist armies

◀ The Japanese were expelled from northeast China largely by the USSR. They handed control to the Chinese Communists, who defeated the Nationalists elsewhere in the country, establishing the People's Republic in October 1949.

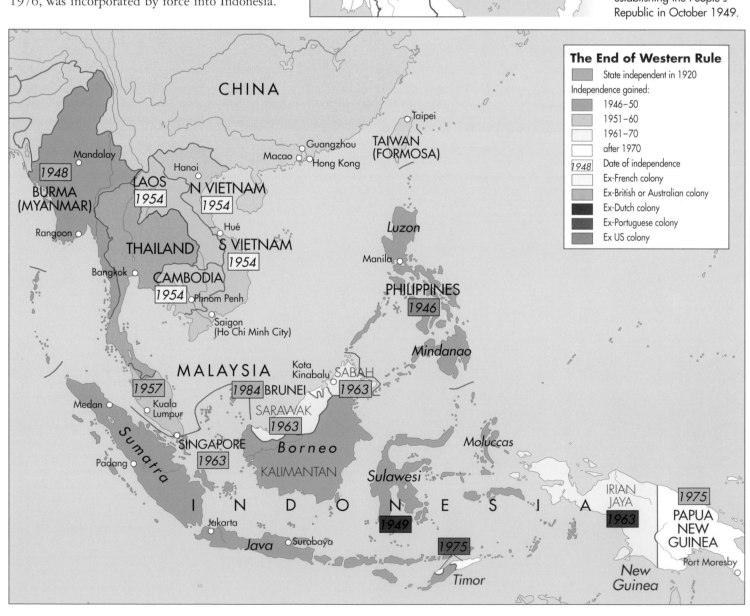

The End of Western Rule

- State independent in 1920

Independence gained:
- 1946–50
- 1951–60
- 1961–70
- after 1970
- *1948* Date of independence
- Ex-French colony
- Ex-British or Australian colony
- Ex-Dutch colony
- Ex-Portuguese colony
- Ex US colony

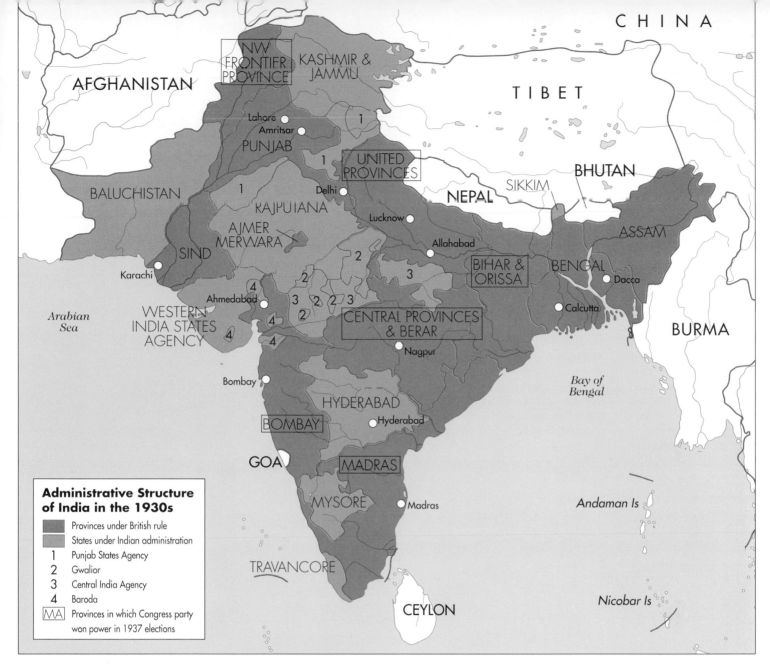

Administrative Structure of India in the 1930s

- ▢ Provinces under British rule
- ▢ States under Indian administration
- **1** Punjab States Agency
- **2** Gwalior
- **3** Central India Agency
- **4** Baroda
- ▢ MA ▢ Provinces in which Congress party won power in 1937 elections

▲ Under British rule, India (with a population of 338 million) was split into administrative regions, some of which were ruled by Indian princes, others by British governors.

◄ After independence Thailand, Malaysia, Singapore, Indonesia and the Philippines set about developing modern industrial economies. With investment from foreign banks and multinational companies, they produced a range of manufactured goods. The industrialisation may have been too rapid, however, for in the late 1990s an economic slump and banking crisis led to social unrest in the region.

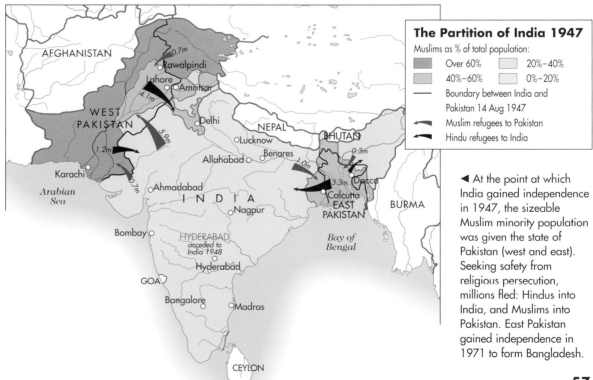

The Partition of India 1947

Muslims as % of total population:
- ▢ Over 60%
- ▢ 40%–60%
- ▢ 20%–40%
- ▢ 0%–20%
- —— Boundary between India and Pakistan 14 Aug 1947
- ➤ Muslim refugees to Pakistan
- ➤ Hindu refugees to India

◄ At the point at which India gained independence in 1947, the sizeable Muslim minority population was given the state of Pakistan (west and east). Seeking safety from religious persecution, millions fled: Hindus into India, and Muslims into Pakistan. East Pakistan gained independence in 1971 to form Bangladesh.

THE MIDDLE EAST AND AFRICA SINCE 1945

Before the Second World War the European powers dominated the Middle East and Africa. In the Middle East they gave up control immediately after the Second World War, but the process of independence in Africa was more gradual. While disputes over territory between newly formed African states have been relatively infrequent, the Middle East has seen several major territorial conflicts: between Israeli Jews and Arab states, Iran and Iraq, and between Iraq and an alliance of Western and Arab states.

▼ The presence of vast oil reserves around the Persian Gulf has enriched the economies of the states that border it and created huge personal fortunes for their ruling families. The Middle East is home to a number of ethnic groups, with Islam the predominant religion.

► Israel was founded in 1947 as a homeland for Jews, who for centuries had been dispersed around Europe and America. The new state displaced the Palestinian Arabs, and has thus aroused continual opposition from its Arab neighbours.

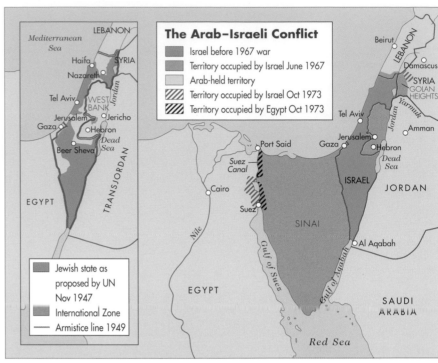

The Arab–Israeli Conflict
- Israel before 1967 war
- Territory occupied by Israel June 1967
- Arab-held territory
- Territory occupied by Israel Oct 1973
- Territory occupied by Egypt Oct 1973

- Jewish state as proposed by UN Nov 1947
- International Zone
- Armistice line 1949

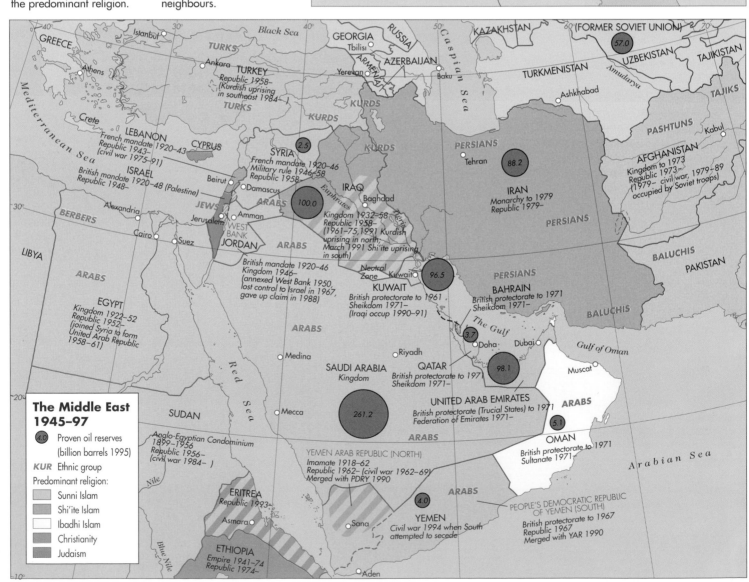

The Middle East 1945–97

- 4.0   Proven oil reserves (billion barrels 1995)
- *KUR*   Ethnic group

Predominant religion:
- Sunni Islam
- Shi'ite Islam
- Ibadhi Islam
- Christianity
- Judaism

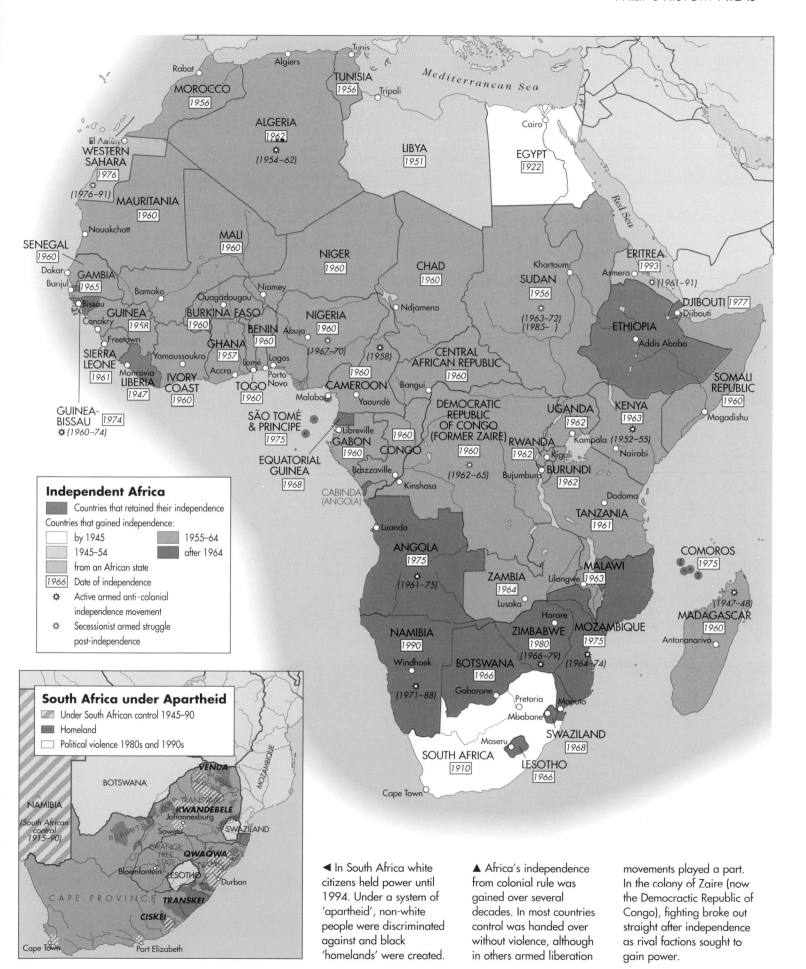

Rabat

Algiers

Tunis

Mediterranean Sea

MOROCCO
1956

TUNISIA
1956

Tripoli

El Aaiún

WESTERN
SAHARA
1976
✷ *(1976–91)*

ALGERIA
1962
✷
(1954–62)

LIBYA
1951

EGYPT
1922

Cairo

Red Sea

MAURITANIA
1960

Nouakchott

SENEGAL
1960

Dakar

GAMBIA
Banjul *1965*

MALI
1960

Bamako

NIGER
1960

Niamey

CHAD
1960

Khartoum

SUDAN
1956

(1963–72)
(1985–)

ERITREA
1993
✷ *(1961–91)*

Asmera

DJIBOUTI *1977*
Djibouti

Ouagadougou

BURKINA FASO
1960

Ndjamena

GUINEA
BISSAU *1974*
✷ *(1960–74)*

Bissau

GUINEA
1958

Conakry

Freetown

SIERRA
LEONE
1961

Monrovia

LIBERIA
1947

Yamoussoukro

GHANA
1957

Accra

IVORY
COAST
1960

TOGO
1960

Lomé

BENIN
1960

Porto
Novo

NIGERIA
1960
✷
(1967–70)

Abuja

Lagos

Malabo

CAMEROON
1960

Yaoundé

Bangui

CENTRAL
AFRICAN REPUBLIC
1960

(1958)
✷

ETHIOPIA

Addis Ababa

SOMALI
REPUBLIC
1960

Mogadishu

SÃO TOMÉ
& PRINCIPE
1975

Libreville

GABON
1960

CONGO
1960

Brazzaville

DEMOCRATIC
REPUBLIC
OF CONGO
(FORMER ZAIRE)
1960
✷
(1962–65)

Kinshasa

UGANDA
1962

Kampala

RWANDA
1962

Kigali

Bujumbura

BURUNDI
1962

KENYA
1963
(1952–55)

Nairobi

Dodoma

TANZANIA
1961

EQUATORIAL
GUINEA
1968

CABINDA
(ANGOLA)

Luanda

ANGOLA
1975
✷
(1961–75)

ZAMBIA
1964

Lusaka

MALAWI
1963

Lilongwe

COMOROS
1975

✷
(1947–48)

MADAGASCAR
1960

Antananarivo

NAMIBIA
1990

Windhoek

(1971–88)

BOTSWANA
1966

Gaborone

ZIMBABWE
1980
(1966–79)

Harare

MOZAMBIQUE
1975
✷
(1964–74)

Maputo

Pretoria

Mbabane

SWAZILAND
1968

Maseru

SOUTH AFRICA
1910

LESOTHO
1966

Cape Town

Independent Africa

▨ Countries that retained their independence

Countries that gained independence:

☐ by 1945   ▨ 1955–64

▨ 1945–54   ▨ after 1964

▨ from an African state

|*1966*| Date of independence

✷   Active armed anti-colonial
     independence movement

✷   Secessionist armed struggle
     post-independence

South Africa under Apartheid

▨ Under South African control 1945–90

▨ Homeland

☐ Political violence 1980s and 1990s

BOTSWANA

MOZAMBIQUE

NAMIBIA
*(South African
control
1915–90)*

VENDA

GAZANKULU

TRANSVAAL

KWANDEBELE

BOPHUTHATSWANA

Johannesburg

Soweto

SWAZILAND

ORANGE
FREE
STATE

QWAQWA

LESOTHO

NATAL

Bloemfontein

Durban

CAPE PROVINCE

TRANSKEI

CISKEI

Cape Town

Port Elizabeth

◄ In South Africa white
citizens held power until
1994. Under a system of
'apartheid', non-white
people were discriminated
against and black
'homelands' were created.

▲ Africa's independence
from colonial rule was
gained over several
decades. In most countries
control was handed over
without violence, although
in others armed liberation

movements played a part.
In the colony of Zaire (now
the Democractic Republic of
Congo), fighting broke out
straight after independence
as rival factions sought to
gain power.

CO-OPERATION AND CONFLICT

Although the period since the Second World War (1939–45) has seemed relatively calm, with the major powers largely avoiding open conflict, in reality war has been waged almost constantly around the world. Some conflicts, such as that between Iran and Iraq in the 1980s, have been between neighbouring states anxious to expand their territory. Others, such as the conflict in Bosnia in the 1990s, have been 'civil wars', with people of the same country fighting for control. The United Nations, founded in 1945, has attempted to keep the peace in around 40 locations worldwide. Member countries have supplied troops, of whom around 750 were killed in action in the first 50 years of operations.

▼ The UN has become involved in peacekeeping operations when one country has invaded another, as in the Middle East, and in countries suffering civil unrest and conflict, as is the case with UN peacekeeping missions to Somalia and Rwanda in the 1990s.

▶ Discrimination against the Catholic minority in Northern Ireland by the Protestant-controlled regional government led, from 1968 onwards, to conflict between para-military groups from both sides of the religious divide, and the deployment of the British army.

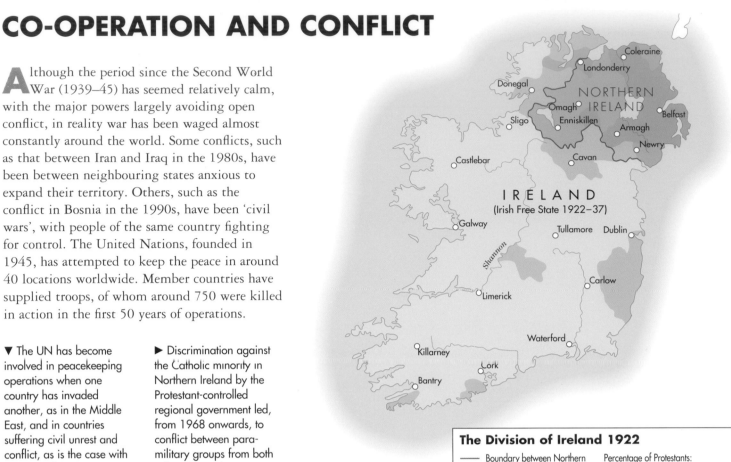

The Division of Ireland 1922

— Boundary between Northern Ireland and Irish Free State, established Dec 1922

Percentage of Protestants:
0–10
10–30
30–50
over 50

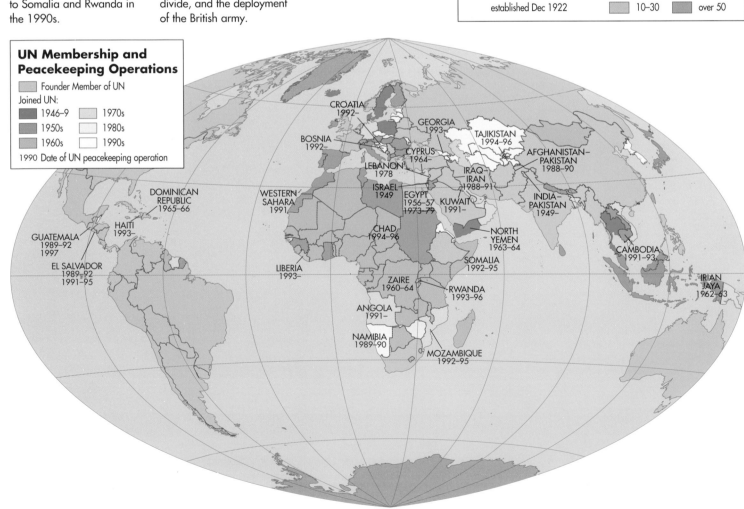

UN Membership and Peacekeeping Operations

Founder Member of UN

Joined UN:
1946–9   1970s
1950s   1980s
1960s   1990s

1990 Date of UN peacekeeping operation

The UN in Bosnia 1994

- Area of Bosnia and Croatia controlled by Serbs
- Area of Bosnia controlled by Bosnian Croats
- Area controlled by Bosnian Muslims
- ○ UN Safe Area established April 1993
- — Boundaries of Bosnia and Croatia
- — Border of former Yugoslavia

The Dayton Peace Agreement 1995

- — Dayton Peace Agreement boundary
- Muslim–Croat Federation
- Bosnian–Serb Federation

▲ Following the collapse of communist rule in 1990, the regions of Slovenia and Croatia both gained independence through armed struggle. Bosnia-Herzegovina, a multi-ethnic area, was torn apart by conflict in 1991–95, as the Bosnian Serbs resisted attempts by the Bosnian Muslims to break away from the control of the Serbian government. The UN failed to bring about peace, which was finally achieved, following NATO direct action, by a team of negotiators at Dayton, Ohio in 1995.

▶ Two wars have arisen since 1980 from Iraq's desire for more oil. The Iran–Iraq War resulted in a ceasefire line little different from the original boundary between the two countries. The Gulf War arose when Iraq invaded oil-rich Kuwait. With the West's oil supplies under threat, a military coalition of the USA, UK, France, Syria, Egypt and Saudia Arabia successfully drove the Iraqis out of Kuwait.

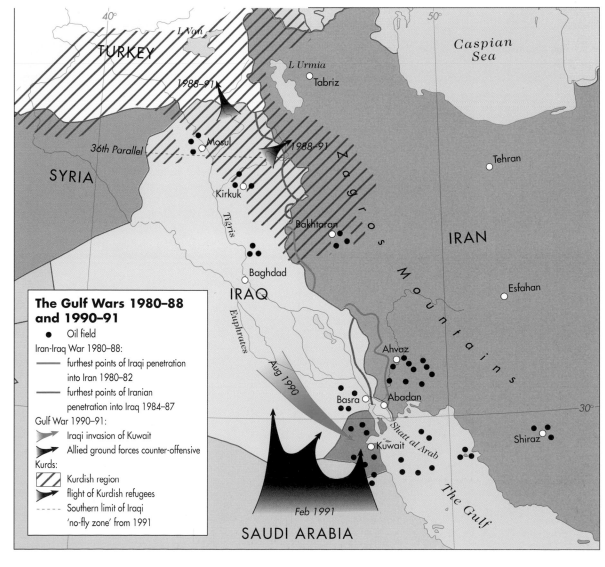

The Gulf Wars 1980–88 and 1990–91

- ● Oil field

Iran-Iraq War 1980–88:
- — furthest points of Iraqi penetration into Iran 1980–82
- — furthest points of Iranian penetration into Iraq 1984–87

Gulf War 1990–91:
- ⮞ Iraqi invasion of Kuwait
- ⮞ Allied ground forces counter-offensive

Kurds:
- ▨ Kurdish region
- ⮞ flight of Kurdish refugees
- --- Southern limit of Iraqi 'no-fly zone' from 1991

INDEX

Main entries for subjects are shown in **bold** type.

INDEX